Illuminating Wit, Inspiring Wisdom

Proverbs
From Around
The World

WOLFGANG MIEDER

PRENTICE HALL PRESS

Printed in the United States of America
10 9 8 7 6 5 4 3 2 1

ISBN 0-7352-0001-7

ATTENTION: CORPORATIONS AND SCHOOLS
Prentice Hall books are available at quantity discounts with bulk purchase for educational, business, or sales promotional use. For information, please write to: Prentice Hall Special Sales, 240 Frisch Court, Paramus, New Jersey 07652. Please supply: title of book, ISBN, quantity, how the book will be used, date needed.

 PRENTICE HALL PRESS
Paramus, NJ 07652

A Simon & Schuster Company

On the World Wide Web at http://www.phdirect.com

Prentice Hall International (UK) Limited, *London*
Prentice Hall of Australia Pty. Limited, *Sydney*
Prentice Hall Canada, Inc., *Toronto*
Prentice Hall Hispanoamericana, S.A., *Mexico*
Prentice Hall of India Private Limited, *New Delhi*
Prentice Hall of Japan, Inc., *Tokyo*
Simon & Schuster Asia Pte. Ltd., *Singapore*
Editora Prentice Hall do Brasil, Ltda., *Rio de Janeiro*

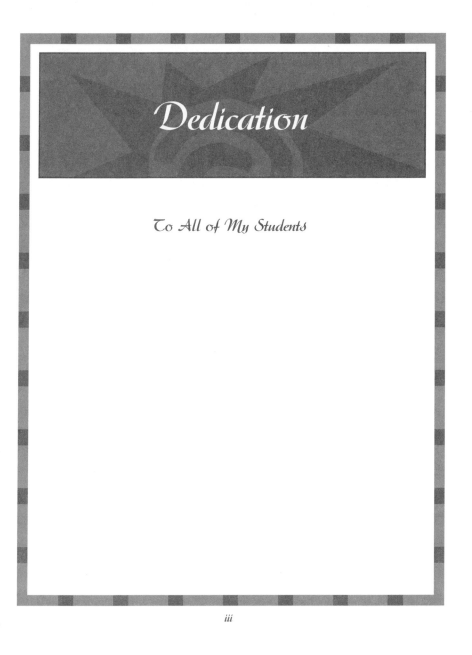

Dedication

To All of My Students

Behold the proverbs of a people.

CARL SANDBURG

Introduction

This collection of proverbs from around the world includes 2000 texts. While a considerable number stem from such major languages as English, Spanish, Chinese, Russian, French, German, and Japanese, there are also numerous proverbs cited from many other languages from all continents: African (Swahili, Yoruba, and others), Indian (Hindi, Tamil, and others), Eastern Europe (Bulgarian, Czech, Serbian, Croatian, etc.), Western Europe (Dutch, Basque, Swedish, among others), the Near East (Egyptian, Iranian, modern Hebrew, etc.), the Far East (Korean, Philippine, Vietnamese, etc.), and also languages from the West Indies and Oceania. Ample examples are also presented from the rich treasure of Yiddish proverbs. The result is a truly international proverb collection with each text cited in English translation.

The proverbs assembled here contain the traditional wisdom of people throughout the world. Each text has been handed down from generation to generation, but while some of the registered proverbs date back to classical antiquity and the wisdom literature of the world's religions, there are also new proverbs of the modern age. Thus ancient proverbs like "One hand washes the other" or "Big fish eat little fish" are today joined by such proverbial insights as "Different strokes for different folks" and "Garbage in, garbage out." They all express in a metaphorical way generalizations about life and nature in general and human behavior in particular.

Proverbs can be defined as concise traditional statements expressing an apparent truth with currency among the folk. Defined more inclusively, proverbs are short, generally known sentences of the folk which contain wisdom, truths, morals, and traditional views in a metaphorical, fixed, and memorizable form and which are handed down orally from generation to generation. There are, of course, some clear "markers" which help to establish that certain short utterances of wisdom or common sense are in fact proverbs. Such markers also assure the memorability and recognizability of the texts as traditional wisdom. In addition to their fixed (and usually oppositional) structure, their relative shortness, and their common use of metaphors, proverbs usually contain some if not all of the following poetic or stylistic features: alliteration: "Many a little makes a mickle," parallelism: "First come, first served," rhyme: "No pains, no gains," ellipsis: "Once bitten, twice shy," personification: "Love laughs at locksmiths," hyperbole: "It is easier for a camel to go through a needle's eye, than for a rich man to enter the kingdom of God" (Matth. 19,24), and paradox: "Absence makes the heart grow fonder." It should be noted that the present collection is purposely restricted to real proverbs. Sententious remarks, familiar quotations, maxims, and aphorisms were intentionally avoided in order to make this book be a "pure" treasure trove of folk wisdom.

Proverbs in actual use are verbal strategies for dealing with social situations. As speech acts they must be viewed as part of the entire communicative performance. This is true for proverbs employed in oral speech but also in their frequent appearance in literary works, the mass media, advertising, popular songs, cartoons, comic strips, etc. Only the use and function of proverbs within particular contexts can determine their specific meanings. While the proverbs in this collection lack the contexts from real-life situations, they become quite significant and alive once they are used as strategic statements that carry the weight and authority of traditional wisdom. Proverbs clearly include various semantic possibilities due to their different functions in varying situations. It is precisely this intangible nature of proverbs which results in their continued and effective use in all modes of human communication.

While glancing at this large number of proverbs, readers must keep in mind the social, cultural, and psycholinguistic significance of contextualized proverbs. Scholars from such varied disciplines as anthropology, art history, ethnology, folklore, history, linguistics, literature, philology, psychology, religion, and sociology, have all looked at proverbs from their particular vantage point. While proverbs can be studied regionally, they are best looked at comparatively through an interdisciplinary, cross-cultural, international, and even global approach. Proverbs are basically used by everyone, everyone is confronted by them, and as verbal nuggets they deserve everyone's attention.

While some proverbs are indigenous to a particular region or country, there are also hundreds of generally known proverbs which cross national boundaries in their geographical distribution. Classical and Biblical proverbs gained wide currency throughout most of the world, and the process of internationalizing certain proverbs can still be observed today. In fact, twentieth-century American proverbs like "A picture is worth a thousand words" and "It takes two to tango" have been accepted in English or as loan translations in numerous foreign cultures through the powerful influence of the mass media. In the present collection, such internationally disseminated proverbs have been registered as "English" proverbs.

Proverbs can be found literally everywhere. In remote areas of the world where literacy has not yet replaced the reliance on oral communication, proverbs are used in their most traditional way as didactic pieces of wisdom. But these seemingly harmless expressions can also take on manipulative power when used in political discourse (debates, speeches, interviews, etc.). The authority of tradition and the inherent claim of expressing truth and wisdom give proverbs in political argumentation a rhetorical power which can make them into manipulative and aggressive weapons. Obviously, proverbs take on similar roles in the vast area of the mass media, from their inclusion in popular songs to the slogans of the advertising world and on to proverbial graffiti. The applicability and adaptability of proverbs seem to be without limit. The moment that a traditional proverb does not appear to be appropriate, its wording is consciously changed while the underlying proverbial structure is maintained. There is thus a steady interplay of tradition and innovation at work here.

The 2000 proverbs of this book assembled from around the world represent in an easily accessible fashion the most important proverbial wisdom from dozens of languages and ethnic groups. While the metaphors might be quite different, the messages of the proverbs under such alphabetically arranged key-words as bread, dog, friendship, love, poverty, reason, women, etc., are often quite similar. Of course, human experiences and behavior differ, and that is reflected in this rich collection. However, many proverbs also show that people everywhere are quite similar as well. The wisdom expressed in this treasure trove of the world's proverbs thus reflects basic, if not universal, human concerns and behavior.

Wolfgang Mieder

A
Whoever says A, must also say B.
GERMAN

Absence
Absence makes the heart grow fonder.
ENGLISH

Abstinence
Abstinence is the best medicine.
INDIAN (TAMIL)

Accomplishment
An accomplishment sticks to a person.
JAPANESE

Accountant
The accountant is clever at numbers, but he is ignorant of his own accounts.
INDIAN (TAMIL)

Admission

Admission by the defendant is worth a hundred witnesses.

HEBREW

Advice

Ask for advice, but do what you think is best.

GREEK

Giving advice to a stupid man is like giving salt to a squirrel.

INDIAN (KASHMIRI)

It is easy to give advice when all goes well.

ITALIAN

Affair

Those who pry into other people's affairs will hear what they do not like.

LIBYAN

Age

Age is a sorry traveling companion.

DANISH

Old age is not a blessing.

RUSSIAN

Agreement
Better a lean agreement than a fat lawsuit.

GERMAN

Anchor
Better lose the anchor than the whole ship.

DUTCH

Anger
Anger is like a thorn in the heart.

YIDDISH

Anger is the only thing to put off till tomorrow.

SLOVAKIAN

The anger of the prudent never shows.

BURMESE

Animal
A large animal is nice but difficult to feed.

AFRICAN (HAUSA)

Ant
An ant is over six feet tall when measured by its own foot-rule.

SLOVENIAN

Many ants kill a camel.

TURKISH

Anvil

A good anvil is not afraid of the hammer.

GREEK

One must be either anvil or hammer.

FRENCH

Appearance

Appearances aren't everything.

AMERICAN

Appetite

Appetite comes with eating.

FRENCH

It is difficult to satisfy one's appetite by painting pictures of cakes.

CHINESE

Apple

An apple a day keeps the doctor away.

ENGLISH

Sour apples must also be eaten.

ESTONIAN

The apple doesn't fall far from the tree.

GERMAN

Archer

The archer that shoots badly has a lie ready.

SPANISH

Armpit

One armpit cannot hold two watermelons.

TURKISH

Arrow

The arrow that has left the bow never returns.

IRANIAN

Ashes

Ashes fly back in the face of him that throws them.

AFRICAN (YORUBA)

Ass

A contented ass enjoys a long life.

PORTUGUESE

An ass is but an ass, though laden with gold.

ENGLISH

Do not load the ass with more than it can carry.

MALTESE

Assertion

Assertion is no proof.

GERMAN

Auction

At an auction keep your mouth shut.

SPANISH

Authority

Authority does not depend on age.

AFRICAN (OVAMBO)

Ax

An ax without a handle does not cut firewood.

AFRICAN (SWAHILI)

Axle

If you don't grease the axle, you won't be able to travel.

RUSSIAN

Baby

Kissing the baby touches the mother.

THAI

Back

Not all who turn their backs are running away.

SWEDISH

The ready back gets all the loads.

LATVIAN

Bad

If you can't endure the bad, you'll not live to witness the good.

YIDDISH

Bag

An old rice bag is ugly, but the thing inside is beautiful.

AFRICAN (KPELLE)

Bagel

If you eat your bagel, you'll have nothing in your pocket but the hole.

YIDDISH

Bait

The bait hides the hook.

ENGLISH

Baking

It is bad baking without flour and water.

GERMAN

Banana

Not every long thing is a banana, nor is every round thing a walnut.

LEBANESE

Bargain

A bargain is a bargain.

ENGLISH

Let your bargain suit your purse.

IRISH

Barrel

There is plenty of sound in an empty barrel.

RUSSIAN

Basket

A basket cannot dam a stream for long.
CHINESE

What fills the small basket does not fill the large one.
AFRICAN (BEMBA)

Battle

Whoever is well prepared has half won the battle.
PORTUGUESE

To win the battle is easy; to secure the victory, difficult.
KOREAN

Bean

One cannot get beans out of wild melons.
AFRICAN (OVAMBO)

Bear (noun)

Don't sell the bearskin before the bear is dead.
DUTCH

Whoever has taken the bear into the boat must cross
over with him.
SWEDISH

Bear (verb)

What was hard to bear is sweet to remember.
PORTUGUESE

Beard

It is not the beard that makes the philosopher.

ENGLISH

Beauty

Beauty and folly are often companions.

FRENCH

Beauty is but skin deep.

ENGLISH

Beauty will fade, but not goodness.

PHILIPPINE

Beauty will not make the pot boil.

IRISH

Bed

As you make your bed, so you must lie on it.

ENGLISH

Better a bed of wood than a bier of gold.

RUSSIAN

Early to bed and early to rise, makes a man healthy and wealthy and wise.

ENGLISH

Even a golden bed does not help a sick person.

ESTONIAN

Bee

One bee is better than a thousand flies.
SPANISH

The wise bee does not sip from a flower that has fallen.
CHINESE

Beetle

The beetle is a beauty in the eyes of its mother.
EGYPTIAN

Beggar

A bashful beggar has an empty wallet.
HUNGARIAN

A beggar who begs from another beggar will never get rich.
JAMAICAN

Beginning

A good beginning is half the work.
IRISH

The beginning is good if the end is good.
PHILIPPINE

Belief

Belief is simpler than investigation.
SLOVENIAN

Bell

A good bell is heard far, a bad one still farther.

FINNISH

One cannot ring the bells and walk in the procession.

FRENCH

Belly

A fat belly did not invent gun powder.

GREEK

A full belly is deaf to learning.

RUSSIAN

An empty belly knows no songs.

GREEK

The hungry belly and the full belly do not walk the same road.

JAMAICAN

Bench

One sits best on one's own bench.

NORWEGIAN

Bird

A bird in the hand is worth two in the bush.

ENGLISH

A caged bird longs for the clouds.

JAPANESE

As the old birds sing, the young ones twitter.

GERMAN

Birds of a feather flock together.

ENGLISH

If you want a bird and a cage, buy the cage first.

AMERICAN

It is a brave bird that makes its nest in the cat's ear.

INDIAN (HINDI)

Little by little the bird builds its nest.

FRENCH

The bird can drink much, but the elephant drinks more.

AFRICAN (WOLOF)

The bird which escapes from the cage never wants to come back.

VIETNAMESE

The early bird catches the worm.

ENGLISH

Young birds do not fly too far.

JAMAICAN

Birth

At birth we bring nothing, at death we take away nothing.
CHINESE

Birth is the remedy for death.
AFRICAN (HAUSA)

Bit (bridle)

A golden bit makes none the better horse.
ITALIAN

Bit (little)

Better a bit in the morning than fast all day.
SCOTTISH

Bitten

Once bitten, twice shy.
ENGLISH

Bitterness

If there's bitterness in the heart, sugar in the mouth won't make life sweeter.
YIDDISH

Black

Black will not become white, nor bitter sweet.
INDIAN (TAMIL)

You can't wash the black off a black dog.

RUSSIAN

Blade

No blade is sharp enough when it strikes stone.

PHILIPPINE

Blanket

A big blanket makes a man sleep late.

JAMAICAN

Blessing

A blessing does not fill the stomach.

IRISH

Blind (adjective)

None are so blind as those that will not see.

ENGLISH

Blind (people)

When the blind leads the blind, both fall into the ditch.

ENGLISH

Blister

Whoever gets blisters from the hoe handle will not die
of hunger.

AFRICAN (SWAHILI)

Block

As the block, so the chip.

RUSSIAN

Blood

Blood boils without fire.

SPANISH

Blood comes from much scratching.

INDIAN (KASHMIRI)

Blood is thicker than water.

ENGLISH

You can't get blood out of a stone.

ENGLISH

Blossom

One blossom doesn't make a spring.

ARMENIAN

Blow (noun)

As the blow, so the pain.

LATVIAN

Blow (verb)

One cannot blow and swallow at the same time.

SPANISH

Boaster

Believe a boaster as you would a liar.
ITALIAN

The boaster gets stuck in the mud.
YIDDISH

Boat

A boat doesn't go forward if everyone is rowing his own way.
AFRICAN (SWAHILI)

Body

Better a sick body than an ignorant mind.
GREEK

Where the body wants to rest, there the legs must carry it.
POLISH

Bone

A bone is more valuable to a dog than a pearl.
PHILIPPINE

Big bones are not cooked in the same pot.
AFRICAN (OVAMBO)

You can't get fat from a dry bone.
CHINESE

Book

A load of books does not equal one good teacher.

CHINESE

It would be a very big book that contained all the maybes
uttered in a day.

FRENCH

Boot

An old boot and an old friend are the most dear.

POLISH

Two boots make a pair.

RUSSIAN

Borrower

Neither a borrower nor lender be.

ENGLISH

Bottle

With a bottle and a girl one does not count the hours.

POLISH

Bow (archery)

The tightly strung bow will relax in time.

JAPANESE

Bow (ship)

If the bow sinks, the stern follows.

PHILIPPINE

Bowel

What is true of the buffalo's bowels is true of the cow's bowels.

VIETNAMESE

Bowl

You can't have more in the bowl than you have in the pot.

YIDDISH

Boy

Boys will be boys.

ENGLISH

Send a boy where he wants to go and you'll see his best pace.

AFRICAN (HAUSA)

While the boy is small, you can see the man.

CHINESE

Bracelet

One bracelet will not jingle.

AFRICAN (HAUSA)

Brain

All the brains are not in one head.
ITALIAN

The brains are not in the beard.
INDIAN (HINDI)

Branch

A crooked branch has a crooked shadow.
JAPANESE

The branch of one tree will not stick to another.
INDIAN (TAMIL)

There is often a withered branch on a green tree.
NORWEGIAN

Bread

A piece of bread in one's pocket is better than a feather
in one's hat.
SWEDISH

Better bread with water than cake with trouble.
RUSSIAN

Eat bread at pleasure, drink wine by measure.
FRENCH

Make bread while the oven is hot.
IRANIAN

When you have bread, do not look for cake.

P O L I S H

Whose bread I eat, his song I sing.

G E R M A N

Without bread and wine even love will pine.

F R E N C H

Breast

A pair of women's breasts has more pulling power than a pair of oxen.

M E X I C A N

Nobody will beat his own breast with a stone.

P H I L I P P I N E

Brevity

Brevity is the soul of wit.

E N G L I S H

Brew

If you brew well, you will drink the better.

S C O T T I S H

Bribe

Bribe is the enemy of justice.

A F R I C A N   (S W A H I L I)

Bribery
Bribery can split a stone.
IRISH

Bricklayer
Too many bricklayers make a lopsided house.
CHINESE

Bride
A fair bride needs little finery.
NORWEGIAN

No bride is ugly on her wedding day.
HEBREW

Bridge
Build golden bridges for the flying foe.
GERMAN

Never cross a bridge till you come to it.
ENGLISH

When the bridge is gone the narrowest plank becomes precious.
HUNGARIAN

Broom

New brooms sweep clean.

ENGLISH

You cannot be a broom and remain clean.

HEBREW

Broth

Fat broth cannot be made of nothing.

FRENCH

Brother

Brothers and sisters are like hands and feet.

VIETNAMESE

With your brother eat and drink, but have no business.

ALBANIAN

Bubble

Every bubble bursts.

POLISH

Buck

An old buck has still horns.

LATVIAN

Bucket

Don't throw away the old bucket until you know whether the
new one holds water.

SWEDISH

Every day the bucket goes to the well, but some day the bottom
must drop out.

JAMAICAN

Bud

All the buds upon a bush do not blossom.

INDIAN (KASHMIRI)

It's the bud that makes the gourd.

AFRICAN (HAUSA)

Buffalo

A buffalo does not feel the weight of his own horns.

INDIAN (HINDI)

What is good for the buffalo is good for the cow.

VIETNAMESE

Bug

The best way to put an end to the bugs is to set fire to the bed.

MEXICAN

Build
What you build easily will fall quickly.
SLOVENIAN

Building
A building of sand falls as you build.
AFRICAN (FULANI)

A building without foundation is soon demolished.
TURKISH

Bull
It is easy to threaten a bull from a window.
ITALIAN

Take good care of the bull if you wish him to plough
well for you.
GREEK

Bun
Half a bun in the hand is better than a whole bun in the shop.
AFRICAN (SWAHILI)

Burden

A voluntary burden is no burden.

ITALIAN

Everyone lays a burden on the willing horse.

IRISH

The heaviest burden is an empty pocket.

YIDDISH

Burial

When the burial day is at your door, you do not pick and choose
your grave diggers.

JAMAICAN

Bush

An ill bush is better than no shelter.

SCOTTISH

One beats the bush, and another catches the bird.

GERMAN

Business

Drive your business, let not that drive you.

AMERICAN

Everybody's business is nobody's business.

ENGLISH

Never do business with a relative.

TURKISH

Butter

All is not butter that comes from the cow.

ITALIAN

They that have much butter, may lay it thick on their bread.

SCOTTISH

Butterfly

The butterfly often forgets it was a caterpillar.

SWEDISH

The butterfly that flies among the thorns will tear its wings.

AFRICAN (JABO)

Button

For a big button, a big buttonhole.

PHILIPPINE

You cannot sew buttons on your neighbor's mouth.

RUSSIAN

Buy

Buy what you do not need, soon you will sell what you need.

CZECH

It is good to buy when another wants to sell.

ITALIAN

Who buys cheap pays twice.

SLOVAKIAN

Buyer

Buyers want a hundred eyes, sellers only one.

GERMAN

There are more foolish buyers than foolish sellers.

FRENCH

Bygone

Let bygones be bygones.

ENGLISH

Cabbage

In the far off field the cabbages are fine.

GREEK

It is not enough to have cabbage, one must have something to grease it.

FRENCH

Cake

One can get sick of cake, but never of bread.

RUSSIAN

You can't eat the rice cake in a picture.

JAPANESE

Calamity

One calamity is better than a thousand counsels.

TURKISH

Calf

A calf is not found under an ox.

ARMENIAN

Better my own ordinary calf than golden calves of others.

KOREAN

The calf belongs to the owner of the cow.

IRISH

The gentle calf sucks all the cows.

PORTUGUESE

Camel

The camel carries the burden, the dog does the panting.

TURKISH

The camel does not see its own hump.

ARMENIAN

Candle

Burn a candle at both ends, and it will not last long.

SCOTTISH

If you wall up a candle with boards, it will not shine.

PHILIPPINE

Canoe

Paddle your own canoe.

AMERICAN

Captain

A wise captain carries more ballast than sail.

JAMAICAN

Many captains sink the ship.

GREEK

Caravan

A caravan does not turn back at the howling of a dog.

TURKISH

They don't unload the caravan for one lame donkey.

IRANIAN

Card

A pack of cards is the devil's prayer book.

GERMAN

Care

Care, and not fine stables, make a good horse.

DANISH

Career

The career of falsehood is short.

PASHTO

Carpenter

A carpenter is known by his chips.

ENGLISH

Carriage

If the carriage be not greased, it does not move on.

TURKISH

Cart

Creaking carts last the longest.

DUTCH

If you are sitting on his cart you must sing his song.

RUSSIAN

Case

A good case is not difficult to state.

AFRICAN (ASHANTI)

Cask

Empty casks make the most noise.

FRENCH

Every cask smells of the wine it contains.

SPANISH

Castle

The higher the castle the nearer to the lightning.

RUSSIAN

Cat

A cat is a lion to a mouse.

ALBANIAN

All cats are grey in the dark.

ENGLISH

An old cat likes young mice.

GREEK

Cat and mouse cannot be neighbors long.

AFRICAN (OVAMBO)

It is better to feed one cat than many mice.

NORWEGIAN

When the cat and mouse agree, the grocer is ruined.

IRANIAN

When the cat has gone, the rats come out to stretch themselves.

CHINESE

When the cat's away the mice will play.

ENGLISH

Cattle

If the cattle are scattered the tiger seizes them.

BURMESE

Cause

Make the best of a bad cause.

SCOTTISH

Caution

Better caution at first than tears afterwards.

YIDDISH

Much caution does no harm.

PORTUGUESE

Change

A change of work is as good as a rest.

IRISH

Change of masters, change of manners.

SCOTTISH

Character

Character is always corrupted by prosperity.

ICELANDIC

Charity

Charity begins at home.

ENGLISH

Charm

Charm is better than beauty.

YIDDISH

Chatter

Much chatter, little wit.

PORTUGUESE

Cheapness

Cheapness costs dearly.

MEXICAN

Cheese

Cheese and bread make the cheeks red.

GERMAN

Cheesecake

You can't make cheesecakes out of snow.

YIDDISH

Cherish

Cherish what you have and struggle for better.

GREEK

Chicken

Do not eat your chicken and throw its feathers in the front yard.

AFRICAN (KPELLE)

My chicken is good, but my neighbor's looks better.

RUMANIAN

Chief

A chief is known by his subjects.

HAWAIIAN

Child (see children)

A burnt child dreads the fire.

ENGLISH

A child learns quicker to talk than to be silent.

NORWEGIAN

A child with seven nannies often has an eye missing.

RUSSIAN

Every mother's child is handsome.

GERMAN

It is too late to cover the well when the child is drowned.

DANISH

Spare the rod and spoil the child.

ENGLISH

The child of a snake is also a snake.
AFRICAN (BEMBA)

Childhood
Childhood is a crown of roses, old age a crown of thorns.
HEBREW

Children (see child)
Better have many children than many riches.
VIETNAMESE

Children and fools speak the truth.
ENGLISH

Children should be seen and not heard.
ENGLISH

Children take after their parents.
MALTESE

Small children eat porridge, big ones eat their parents' hearts.
CZECH

The children of the same mother do not always agree.
AFRICAN (WOLOF)

Chimney
It is easier to build two chimneys, than to maintain one.
ENGLISH

Chip

Chips don't fall without being hacked from the tree.

SWEDISH

Little chips kindle the fire, and big logs sustain it.

PORTUGUESE

Choice

No choice is also a choice.

YIDDISH

There is small choice in rotten apples.

ENGLISH

Circumstance

Circumstances alter cases.

ENGLISH

Cleanliness

Cleanliness is next to godliness.

ENGLISH

Cloak

Arrange your cloak as the wind blows.

FRENCH

Where you lost your cloak, seek it.

SPANISH

Cloth

Measure your cloth seven times, you can cut it but once.

RUSSIAN

You cannot take white cloth out of a tub full of indigo.

CHINESE

Clothes

Borrowed clothes are either too tight or too loose.

PHILIPPINE

Cloud

All clouds do not rain.

DUTCH

Every cloud has a silver lining.

ENGLISH

Coat

As the coat, so the lining.

LATVIAN

Though your coat is dirty, you do not burn it.

AFRICAN (OJI)

Cock

Every cock is brave on his own dunghill.
ENGLISH

Two cocks do not crow from the same roof.
AFRICAN (ANNANG)

Cockroach

The cockroach never wins its cause when the chicken is judge.
HAITIAN

Coconut

A bad coconut spoils the good ones.
AFRICAN (SWAHILI)

Color

The color does not come off a zebra.
AFRICAN (OVAMBO)

Come

First come, first served.
ENGLISH

Whoever comes first, grinds first.
GERMAN

Community

Every community has its own customs and traditions.

PHILIPPINE

Company

Better to be alone than in bad company.

SPANISH

Cheerful company shortens the miles.

GERMAN

Comparison

Comparisons are odious.

ENGLISH

Compromise

A lean compromise is better than a fat lawsuit.

DUTCH

Cone

A fir cone does not fall far from the tree.

ESTONIAN

Confession

The confession of a fault removes half its guilt.

INDIAN (TAMIL)

Confidence

Confidence is half the victory.

HEBREW

Too much confidence is destructive.

PHILIPPINE

Conscience

A clear conscience sleeps during thunder.

JAMAICAN

A good conscience is a soft pillow.

GERMAN

Contract

No one makes contracts with God.

RUSSIAN

Conversation

The conversation between husband and wife no one knows
about.

AFRICAN (ASHANTI)

Cook

All are not cooks who carry long knives.

DUTCH

Too many cooks spoil the broth.

ENGLISH

Copper

Do not throw away your copper for the sake of gold's glitter.

AFRICAN (SWAHILI)

Cord

When the cord is tightest it is nearest snapping.

DANISH

Cork

The cork is always bigger than the mouth of the bottle.

ESTONIAN

Corn

One reaps the same corn one sows.

FINNISH

You can't grow corn on the ceiling.

YIDDISH

Corner

The corner of the house may be explored and seen, but not the corner of the heart.

AUSTRALIAN (MAORI)

Cost

It doesn't cost anything to ask.
RUSSIAN

What costs little is little esteemed.
ENGLISH

Cottage

A thatched cottage with love is still better than a tile-roofed
castle without it.
VIETNAMESE

Better inside a cottage than outside a castle.
WELSH

Cotton

Cotton cannot play with fire.
TURKISH

Counsel

Counsel after action is like rain after harvest.
DANISH

Good counsel comes overnight.
GERMAN

Where there's counsel, there's also love.
RUSSIAN

Country

A country may go to ruin but its mountains and streams remain.

JAPANESE

So many countries, so many customs.

ENGLISH

Couple

Every couple is not a pair.

ENGLISH

Courage

Courage beats the enemy.

PHILIPPINE

Who has no courage must have legs.

ITALIAN

Courtesy

Courtesy that is all on one side cannot last long.

FRENCH

Courtship

A short courtship is the best courtship.

MANX

Cousin

Too many cousins ruin the shopkeeper.

JAMAICAN

Cover

According to your cover stretch your legs.

LIBYAN

Cow

A cow does not know the value of its tail until it is cut off.

AFRICAN (SWAHILI)

After dark every cow is black.

SLOVAKIAN

An old cow does not remember having been a calf.

FINNISH

Many a good cow has but a bad calf.

MANX

Milk the cow, but don't pull off the udder.

DUTCH

The cows that low most give the least milk.

GERMAN

You cannot sell the cow and sup the milk.

SCOTTISH

Coward

Cowards die often.
ENGLISH

Nobody is a coward when his rights are trampled upon.
PHILIPPINE

The real coward runs even if he is not wounded.
PHILIPPINE

Crab

A crab does not give birth to a bird.
AFRICAN (ASHANTI)

The crab that lies always in its hole is never fat.
MANX

Cradle

What is learned in the cradle lasts till the grave.
FRENCH

Craft

Be not ashamed of your craft.
GERMAN

Crane

A thousand cranes in the air are not worth one sparrow
in the fist.

EGYPTIAN

When the crane attempts to dance with the horse it
gets broken bones.

DANISH

Creak

That which creaks must be oiled.

LATVIAN

Credit

Credit is better than ready money.

GERMAN

Credit is invisible fortune.

JAPANESE

Creditor

Creditors have better memories than debtors.

ENGLISH

Crime

Crime cries out for punishment.

PHILIPPINE

Crocodile

A crocodile cares not whether the water is deep or shallow.

INDIAN (TAMIL)

Crop

A good crop, sell early; a bad crop, sell late.

RUSSIAN

Crow

A crow does not lay dove's eggs.

GREEK

Every crow thinks its own young one prettiest.

SCOTTISH

One crow does not peck out another's eyes.

GERMAN

Crown

A crown is no cure for the headache.

DUTCH

Crumb

Where there are crumbs there will be mice.

RUSSIAN

Crust

Even a crust is bread.

FINNISH

Cry

Much cry and little wool.

ENGLISH

Cuckoo

One cuckoo doesn't make the spring.

GREEK

Cure (noun)

The cure for old age is the grave.

RUSSIAN

The only cure for sorrow is to kill it with patience.

IRISH

Cure (verb)

What can't be cured must be endured.

ENGLISH

Curiosity
Curiosity killed the cat.
AMERICAN

Currant
One can't get currants without stalks.
PASHTO

Custom
Custom and law are sisters.
SLOVAKIAN

When you enter a village, observe its customs.
KOREAN

Customer
The customer is always right.
AMERICAN

Cut
Don't cut without measuring.
IRANIAN

Dance (noun)
The dance is good when the music is good.
PHILIPPINE

Dance (verb)
Not every one that dances is glad.
FRENCH

Dancing
More belongs to dancing than a pair of fine shoes.
ICELANDIC

Danger
A common danger produces unity.
SLOVAKIAN

Danger past and God forgotten.
SCOTTISH

Shun danger and it will shun you.
IRISH

There's danger in delay.
AMERICAN

Daughter

After the daughter is married, then come sons-in-law in plenty.
FRENCH

Daughters are fragile ware.
JAPANESE

He that would the daughter win must with the mother
first begin.
ENGLISH

Day

A day is long, but a lifetime is short.
RUSSIAN

Don't think of the shortness of the day, but of the length
of the year.
MALAGASY

Every day has its own fate.
SLOVENIAN

Every day is not Sunday.
ENGLISH

One day teaches the other.
LITHUANIAN

Praise a fine day at night.
GERMAN

Dead
Don't bear a grudge against the dead.
JAPANESE

Death
Death combs us all with the same comb.
SWEDISH

Death is the grand leveller.
ENGLISH

Death takes the poor man's cow and the rich man's child.
FRENCH

No matter how long one may live, the day of death will come.
INDIAN (TAMIL)

Debt

A debt is not paid with words.

TURKISH

Better go to bed without supper than to live with debts.

CZECH

You cannot pay a debt with a sigh.

YIDDISH

Deed

A good deed bears interest.

ESTONIAN

A good deed is the best prayer.

MEXICAN

Deeds, not words.

ENGLISH

One deed is worth a thousand speeches.

AMERICAN

Deer

Whoever chases after a deer will take no notice of hares.

KOREAN

Defect

The defects in the eyelashes are not apparent to the eye.

INDIAN (TAMIL)

Defense

The best defense is a good offense.

AMERICAN

Delay

Delay will lead to ruin.

INDIAN (TAMIL)

Departure

Every departure has an arrival.

TURKISH

Desire

Desire conquers fear.

IRISH

If you have the desire, distance doesn't matter.

PHILIPPINE

Despair

Despair and hope are sisters.

SLOVENIAN

Destiny

All destinies are not alike.

AFRICAN (ASHANTI)

Determination

There is nothing that cannot be achieved by firm determination.

JAPANESE

Devil

It is easy to bid the devil be your guest, but difficult to get rid of him.

DANISH

One devil knows another.

ITALIAN

Talk of the devil and he'll appear.

ENGLISH

The devil take the hindmost.

ENGLISH

Dew

If you rise too early, the dew will wet you.

AFRICAN (WOLOF)

In the ant's house the dew is a flood.

IRANIAN

Diamond

A diamond is a girl's best friend.

AMERICAN

Diamond cut diamond.

ENGLISH

Die

Better to die upright than to live on your knees.

YIDDISH

One has only to die to be praised.

GERMAN

Dike

Where the dike is lowest the water first runs out.

DUTCH

Diligence

Diligence is the mother of success.

ENGLISH

Dinner

Better a good dinner than a fine coat.

FRENCH

If you want your dinner, don't offend the cook.

CHINESE

Dipper
A dipper can't be used for an earpick.
JAPANESE

Disaster
Serious disasters come from small causes.
JAPANESE

Discretion
Discretion is the better part of valor.
ENGLISH

Disease
Diseases come by mountains and leave by driblets.
THAI

When the disease is not known there is no remedy.
BURMESE

Disposition
A good disposition is the best treasure.
INDIAN (TAMIL)

Distance
Distance preserves friendship.
IRANIAN

Distrust

Distrust is poison to friendship.

DANISH

Doctor

Better no doctor at all than three.

POLISH

The doctor has a remedy for everything but poverty.

YIDDISH

There is no doctor on the day of death.

AFRICAN (FULANI)

Dog

A dog that means to bite does not show his teeth.

TURKISH

A noisy dog is not fit for hunting.

INDIAN (TAMIL)

An old dog does not howl at the stump of a tree.

BASQUE

Be a dog ever so quick to start it will not catch a monkey
swarming up a tree.

AFRICAN (FULANI)

Dead dogs don't bite.
DUTCH

Every dog has his day.
ENGLISH

If you play with the dog, he will lick your face.
VIETNAMESE

Let sleeping dogs lie.
ENGLISH

The dog barks and the caravan passes on.
TURKISH

The dog is boldest at home.
NORWEGIAN

Two dogs fight for a bone and a third runs away with it.
GERMAN

You can't teach an old dog new tricks.
ENGLISH

Doing
Whatever is worth doing is worth doing well.
ENGLISH

Dollar

A dollar saved is as good as a dollar earned.

AMERICAN

Donkey

When a donkey is well off he goes dancing on ice.

CZECH

Door

A door must either be open or shut.

FRENCH

Let everyone sweep before his own door.

GERMAN

When one door shuts, a hundred open.

SPANISH

Dream

Dreams are froth.

GERMAN

Dreams go by contraries.

ENGLISH

The dream of the cat is all about the mice.

EGYPTIAN

Drink

A drink is shorter than a story.

IRISH

Drinking

Where there's drinking, there's spilling.

RUSSIAN

Drop

Drop by drop fills the tub.

FRENCH

Many drops make a great flood.

INDIAN (TAMIL)

Dropping

Constant dropping wears the stone.

GERMAN

Drum

It is difficult to beat a drum with a sickle.

AFRICAN (HAUSA)

You can't hide a drum under a blanket.

IRANIAN

Drunkard

There are more old drunkards than old doctors.

FRENCH

Duck

The duck knows where the lake is.

GREEK

Dumpling

Dumplings are better than flowers.

JAPANESE

Dust

Dust does not rise because a dog-flea hops.

BURMESE

Duty

Do your duty and be afraid of none.

AMERICAN

Eagle

Better be an eagle for a day than a rook for a whole year.

RUMANIAN

Eagles don't breed doves.

DUTCH

Ear

Listen with each ear, then do judgment.

MANX

What one whispers in the ear is heard throughout the town.

SWEDISH

Earth

Black earth gives white bread.

SWEDISH

Eat

Eat little, sleep sound.

IRANIAN

To eat one must chew, to speak one must think.

VIETNAMESE

Eating

Eating and drinking wants but a beginning.

SCOTTISH

Eating teaches drinking.

ITALIAN

Echo

The echo knows all languages.

FINNISH

Education

Better education than wealth.

WELSH

Education is light, lack of it is darkness.

RUSSIAN

Eel

To squeeze an eel too hard is the way to lose it.

FRENCH

You cannot hide an eel in a sack.

ENGLISH

Egg

Better an egg today than a hen tomorrow.

ALBANIAN

Don't boil eggs until the hen has laid them.

ESTONIAN

Don't put all your eggs into one basket.

ENGLISH

Eggs are not fried with wind.

LEBANESE

Eggs cannot be unscrambled.

AMERICAN

To eat an egg, you must break the shell.

JAMAICAN

Eggplant

Eggplants do not grow on melon vines.

JAPANESE

Elephant

An elephant does not eat small berries.

AFRICAN (GA)

An elephant is not affected by sunshine or rain.

INDIAN (TAMIL)

An elephant is not burdened by its tusks.

AFRICAN (SHONA)

The elephant does not feel a flea bite.

ITALIAN

Elk

Kill the elk in your youth if you would lie on its skin in your old age.

FINNISH

Embrace

The embrace at meeting is better than that at parting.

EGYPTIAN

End

The end crowns the work.

FRENCH

The end of the journey is reached by moving ahead.

AFRICAN (OVAMBO)

There is an end to every song.
SLOVAKIAN

Endurance
Endurance pierces marble.
MOROCCAN

Enemy
An old enemy never becomes a friend.
GREEK

Better an open enemy than a false friend.
DANISH

Beware of a reconciled enemy.
FRENCH

Engagement
Better to break off an engagement than a marriage.
YIDDISH

Enough
Enough is as good as a feast.
ENGLISH

There was never enough where nothing was left.
SCOTTISH

Envy (noun)

Envy does not enter an empty house.

DANISH

Envy hatches swans from rotten duck eggs.

RUSSIAN

Where there is envy, there is meanness.

GREEK

Equality

Where there is not equality there never can be perfect love.

ITALIAN

Err

To err is human.

ENGLISH

Errand

Errands are small on a spring day.

ICELANDIC

Error

Every error has its excuse.

POLISH

The first error is overlooked.

MANX

Estate

A great estate is not gotten in a few hours.

FRENCH

An estate inherited is the less valued.

PORTUGUESE

Estimate

The estimate made at home does not hold good at the market.

RUMANIAN

Evening

In the evening one may praise the day.

GERMAN

Evil

Evil condoned is evil consented.

MEXICAN

Evil to him that evil thinks.

ENGLISH

Of two evils choose the least.

ENGLISH

Example

A good example is the best sermon.

ENGLISH

Exception
Exceptions prove the rule.
ENGLISH

Exchange
Fair exchange is no robbery.
ENGLISH

Expense
It is the petty expenses that empty the purse.
ITALIAN

Experience
Experience is good, but often dear bought.
SCOTTISH

Experience is the best teacher.
GERMAN

Experience keeps a dear school, but fools will learn in no other.
ENGLISH

Without experience one gains no wisdom.
CHINESE

Expert

Two experts are never on good terms.

AFRICAN (SHONA)

Extreme

Extremes meet.

ENGLISH

Eye

A lax eye spells a broken head.

MALAYSIAN

Four eyes see more than two.

ENGLISH

Not all are asleep who have their eyes shut.

ITALIAN

Some have fine eyes and can't see a jot.

FRENCH

What the eyes do not see the heart does not desire.

RUSSIAN

Eyesight

Eyesight is more powerful than hearsay.

ICELANDIC

Face

A good face needs no paint.

ENGLISH

Better a red face than a black heart.

PORTUGUESE

The face is the mirror of the heart.

JAPANESE

Fact

Facts are stranger than fiction.

AMERICAN

Failure

Failure is the source of success.

JAPANESE

Failure teaches you more than success.

RUSSIAN

Faith
Faith can move mountains.
ENGLISH

Fame
All fame brings envy.
ENGLISH

Fame endures longer than life.
IRISH

Familiarity
Familiarity breeds contempt.
ENGLISH

Family
As the family is, so is the offspring.
RUSSIAN

If a family has an old person in it, it possesses a jewel.
CHINESE

In time of test, family is best.
BURMESE

Farmer
If the farmer fails all will starve.
AMERICAN

The farmer hopes for rain, the traveler for fine weather.

Fashion

What's in fashion will be out of fashion.

Fasting

Fasting is easy with a chicken leg and a half-bottle of wine.

It is easy to preach fasting with a full belly.

Fate

No fate is worse than a life without a love.

Father

Father and mother are the most precious jewels on earth.

Like father, like son.

The father a saint, the son a sinner.

Fault

Don't find fault with what you don't understand.

FRENCH

Faults are thick where love is thin.

ENGLISH

Favor

Favor and gifts disturb justice.

DANISH

To accept a favor is to lose your liberty.

POLISH

Fear

Fear and love do not walk together.

LITHUANIAN

Fear has large eyes.

RUSSIAN

Fear of the grave comes with old age.

AFRICAN (SWAHILI)

Feather

Feather by feather the goose is plucked.

ITALIAN

Fee

No fee, no law.

ENGLISH

Feet (see foot)

Do not stretch your feet beyond your carpet.

LEBANESE

The gardener's feet do no harm to the garden.

SPANISH

Fellow

An unlucky fellow gets hurt on his nose even when he tumbles backward.

KOREAN

Don't kick a fellow when he's down.

AMERICAN

Fence

A fence between makes love more keen.

GERMAN

Good fences make good neighbors.

AMERICAN

Fiber

A single fiber does not make a thread.

CHINESE

Fiddle

The fiddle sings one tune and the bow another.

GREEK

Field

Take care of your field, and your field will take care of you.

GERMAN

The neighbor's field is easy to hoe.

AFRICAN (OVAMBO)

Fight

Don't join in a fight if you have no weapons.

AFRICAN (SWAHILI)

Figure

Figures don't lie.

AMERICAN

Finger

A single finger cannot catch fleas.

HAITIAN

Don't put your finger into too tight a ring.

FRENCH

Fire

A little fire that warms is better than a big fire that burns.

IRISH

Fire and gunpowder do not sleep together.

AFRICAN (ASHANTI)

Fire and straw do not go together.

GREEK

The fire of lust is more fierce than a smoking fire.

INDIAN (TAMIL)

Where there's no fire there's no smoke.

PORTUGUESE

Fish

A small fish is better than a large cockroach.

RUSSIAN

Big fish eat little fish.

ENGLISH

Every little fish expects to become a whale.

DANISH

The fish that escaped is the big one.

CHINESE

The little fish cannot swallow the big fish.

HAWAIIAN

Fist

Don't swing your fists after the fight.

RUSSIAN

Flight

The flight of the eagle will not stop that of the sandfly.

AFRICAN (FULANI)

Flood

A flood is more easily controlled than love.

PHILIPPINE

Every flood has its ebb.

DUTCH

Floor

Let everyone sweep his own floor.

AFRICAN (OVAMBO)

Flour

The flour tastes bitter to the mouse who has had enough.

SLOVAKIAN

Flower

Even the most beautiful flower has its thorns.

PHILIPPINE

Painted flowers are scentless.

GERMAN

Yesterday's lovely flower is but a dream today.

JAPANESE

Fly

A fly does not mind dying in coconut cream.

AFRICAN (SWAHILI)

Big flies break the spider's web.

ITALIAN

Hungry flies bite sore.

ENGLISH

The busy fly is in every man's dish.

SPANISH

Folk

Busy folks are always meddling.

ENGLISH

Little folks are fond of talking about what great folks do.

GERMAN

Some folks are born to be lucky.

AMERICAN

Food

If there is food in the house, a guest is no worry.
PASHTO

The best food is that which fills the belly.
EGYPTIAN

There is no bad food in time of starvation.
PHILIPPINE

Fool

A fool and his money are soon parted.
ENGLISH

A fool grows without rain.
YIDDISH

Advising a fool is like striking cold iron.
GREEK

Every fool wants to give advice.
ITALIAN

Fools rush in where angels fear to tread.
ENGLISH

If a fool could keep silent he would not be a fool.
SWEDISH

The fool plucks at a wasp's nest.
PHILIPPINE

The fool will laugh when drowning.

WELSH

There is no fool like the old fool.

ENGLISH

When a fool has too many roses he plants thorns amongst them.

RUSSIAN

Foolishness

Foolishness grows by itself, no need to sow it.

CZECH

Foot (see feet)

Better slip with the foot than with the tongue.

ITALIAN

The foot that travels the road is the one that is pricked by the thorn.

AFRICAN (JABO)

Ford

First find the ford, then cross the river.

ARMENIAN

Praise the ford when you have crossed it.

IRISH

Fortune

Fortune and misfortune are like the twisted strands of a rope.

JAPANESE

Good fortune closes the eyes, misfortune opens them.

SLOVAKIAN

If fortune turns against you, even jelly breaks your tooth.

IRANIAN

There is no good fortune which is not shadowed by misfortune.

SLOVENIAN

When fortune knocks, open the door.

GERMAN

Fountain

When it dries up, one knows the worth of the fountain.

RUMANIAN

Fox

An old fox does not run twice into the snare.

GERMAN

Nothing falls into the mouth of a sleeping fox.

FRENCH

The fox sits but once on a thorn.

ARMENIAN

When the fox starts preaching, look to your hens.

BASQUE

Freedom

A country's freedom cannot be bought by any amount of gold.

PHILIPPINE

Friend

A fair-weather friend changes with the wind.

SPANISH

A friend in need is a friend indeed.

ENGLISH

An old friend is like a saddled horse.

PASHTO

Correct your friend secretly and praise him publicly.

CZECH

Hold a true friend with both your hands.

AFRICAN (KANURI)

If a friend is honey, do not try to eat all of him.

RUMANIAN

In distress a friend is best.

WELSH

It is easier to visit friends than to live with them.

CHINESE

Old friends and old wine are best.

ENGLISH

Real friends will share even a strawberry.

SLOVAKIAN

Friendship

Friendship is friendship, but money has to be counted.

RUSSIAN

Friendship is the marriage of the soul.

JAPANESE

You can't patch up a torn friendship.

YIDDISH

Frog

A frog in the well knows not the ocean.

JAPANESE

The frog will jump back into the pool although it sits on a golden stool.

DUTCH

You can't catch two frogs with one hand.

CHINESE

Froth

Froth is no beer.

DUTCH

Fruit

Forbidden fruit is sweet.

ENGLISH

Ripe fruit does not remain on the branch.

INDIAN (TAMIL)

There is no fruit from a dry tree.

TURKISH

Frying Pan

He has enough to do who holds the handle of the frying pan.

FRENCH

Fuel

Fuel alone will not light a fire.

CHINESE

Fur

Those with the same fur enter the same hole.

AFRICAN (FULANI)

Furniture

Better a little furniture than an empty house.

DANISH

Future

Whoever has no care for the far future will have sorrow in the near future.

KOREAN

Learn the future by looking at things past.

INDIAN (TAMIL)

Gain

No gains without pains.

Small gains bring great wealth.

Gambler

If you help a gambler, it is as if you throw a hair into the fire.

The gambler is always a loser.

Gambling

Gambling and boasting end in sorrow.

If you believe in gambling, in the end you will sell your house.

Game

It is a bad game where nobody wins.
ITALIAN

The game is not worth the candle.
ENGLISH

Garbage

Garbage in, garbage out.
AMERICAN

Garden

A garden without a fence is like a dog without a tail.
MOROCCAN

Everyone has enough to do in weeding his own garden.
FLEMISH

Garment

Borrowed garments do not fit well.
JAPANESE

Our last garment is made without pockets.
ITALIAN

Gate

A creaking gate hangs long.
ENGLISH

Geese (see goose)

Roast geese don't come flying into your mouth.

DUTCH

Gem

Even a gem has a flaw.

KOREAN

General

A general of a defeated army should not talk of tactics.

JAPANESE

There cannot be a general without soldiers.

TURKISH

Generation

One generation opens the road upon which another generation travels.

Generosity

The best generosity is that which is quick.

EGYPTIAN

Gift

Gifts can soften even stone.

PHILIPPINE

Gifts cripple the law, and grease makes the wheel go round.

FINNISH

The best gifts are those which expect no return.

NORWEGIAN

Gift Horse

Don't look a gift horse in the mouth.

ENGLISH

Girl

A girl draws more than a rope.

SPANISH

Even the wisest girl will yield to the boy who perseveres
in his wooing.

VIETNAMESE

Girls will be girls.

AMERICAN

Give

Give a little and you gain a lot.

PASHTO

It is better to give than to receive.

ENGLISH

Glacier

It is no use trying to tug the glacier backwards.

TIBETAN

Goat

A goat is not easy to fence in.

NORWEGIAN

The goat eats where it is tied.

FINNISH

Gold

All that glitters is not gold.

ENGLISH

Gold does not buy everything.

ITALIAN

Gold without wisdom is but clay.

SLOVAKIAN

Goods

From peddling small goods on the streets you don't make big fortunes.

YIDDISH

Ill-gotten goods seldom prosper.

GERMAN

Goose (see geese)
A goose drinks as much as a gander.
DANISH

A wild goose never lays a tame egg.
ENGLISH

Gossip
Gossip needs no carriage.
RUSSIAN

It is easier to close a river than to stop gossip.
PHILIPPINE

Government
Government is best which governs least.
AMERICAN

Grain
Grain by grain the hen fills her crop.
SPANISH

One grain suffices to test a whole pot of boiled rice.
INDIAN (TAMIL)

Grape

If you can't get grapes get an apple.
RUSSIAN

The sweetest grapes hang highest.
GERMAN

Grass

No grass grows in the marketplace.
ENGLISH

No grass grows under the stone that is often moved.
SWEDISH

The grass is always greener on the other side of the fence.
AMERICAN

Grief

Grief and joy are a revolving wheel.
INDIAN (TAMIL)

The most recent grief is the heaviest to bear.
IRISH

Ground

The best ground has weeds.
JAMAICAN

Grudge

A grudge is not held against a dead person.
AFRICAN (ZULU)

Guest

A guest, like a fish, stinks the third day.
DUTCH

Guests should not forget to go home.
SWEDISH

Seven days is the length of a guest's life.
BURMESE

Gunpowder

Gunpowder and fire do not agree.
AFRICAN (GA)

Gutter

Better repair the gutter than the whole house.
PORTUGUESE

Habit

A habit that has started at three will continue till eighty.

KOREAN

Old habits have deep roots.

NORWEGIAN

Hair

A hair of the dog that bit you.

ENGLISH

Even a thread of hair has its shadow.

RUMANIAN

One hair of a woman draws more than a team of oxen.

ENGLISH

Hammer

A golden hammer breaks an iron gate.

GERMAN

It is better to be the hammer than the anvil.

RUSSIAN

Hand

Cold hands, warm heart.
GERMAN

If you applaud with one hand it will not be heard.
AFRICAN (OVAMBO)

Many hands make light work.
ENGLISH

One hand cannot hold two watermelons.
LEBANESE

One hand washes the other.
ENGLISH

The idle hand gets nothing.
MANX

Handsome

Handsome is as handsome does.
ENGLISH

Happiness

If you have happiness, don't use it all up.
CHINESE

There is no happiness without jealousy.
RUSSIAN

Hare

A hare is not caught by sitting down.

AFRICAN (HAUSA)

In small woods may be caught large hares.

DUTCH

Harpoon

A small harpoon can kill a whale.

PHILIPPINE

Haste

Haste makes waste.

ENGLISH

Marry in haste and repent at leisure.

DUTCH

Hat

Hat in hand goes through the whole land.

GERMAN

You can't make a hat out of a pig's tail.

YIDDISH

Hatchet

A small hatchet fells a great oak.

PORTUGUESE

Hawk

Better a hawk in the hand than two in flight.
ICELANDIC

It's hard to catch hawks with empty hands.
DUTCH

Hay

Make hay while the sun shines.
ENGLISH

Head

A wise head keeps a shut mouth.
IRISH

It is hard to put many heads under one hat.
SWEDISH

It is no time to bow when the head is off.
SCOTTISH

The head suffers because of the tongue.
SLOVAKIAN

Two heads are better than one.
ENGLISH

What one does not have in the head, one must have in the legs.
GERMAN

Headache

Neither hat nor crown help against headache.

SWEDISH

Health

Health is better than wealth.

ENGLISH

Heart

A happy heart is better than a full purse.

ITALIAN

Faint heart never won fair lady.

ENGLISH

If the heart be stout, a mouse can lift an elephant.

TIBETAN

It's a poor heart that never rejoices.

ENGLISH

The heart has no window.

RUSSIAN

When the heart is in love, beauty is of no account.

PASHTO

Hearth
A hearth of your own is worth gold.
GERMAN

Heir
Many heirs make small portions.
GERMAN

Hell
Hell is paved with good intentions.
ENGLISH

Helm
It is easy to sit at the helm in fine weather.
DANISH

Help
A little help does a great deal.
FRENCH

Hen
A hen carried far is heavy.
IRISH

Hens that cackle much lay few eggs.
ESTONIAN

It never goes well when the hen crows.

RUSSIAN

The hen lays an egg, and the cock feels pain in his bottom.

MOROCCAN

Hero

Heroes cannot stand side by side.

JAPANESE

No man is a hero to his valet.

ENGLISH

Herring

Don't cry herrings till they are in the net.

DUTCH

Every herring must hang by its own gills.

ENGLISH

Hesitate

He who hesitates is lost.

ENGLISH

Hide

You can't get two hides from one ox.

RUSSIAN

Hill

Every hill has its valley.
ITALIAN

Hills are green afar off.
ENGLISH

Hinge

The hinge of a door is never crowded with insects.
CHINESE

Hint

A hint is about as good as a kick to some people.
AMERICAN

Hippopotamus

It is the mother hippopotamus which shows the little one how
to dive.
AFRICAN (BEMBA)

Hog

If you saw what the hog ate, you would never eat hog meat.
JAMAICAN

Hole

A hole is more easily patched than a crack.

PHILIPPINE

Holiday

It will not do to keep holidays before they come.

FRENCH

Home

East or west, home is best.

DUTCH

Home is where the heart is.

AMERICAN

My home is my castle.

ENGLISH

Honey

Honey is sweet, but the bee stings.

ENGLISH

Where the honey is spread there will the flies gather.

INDIAN (HINDI)

You cannot handle honey without licking your fingers.

SLOVENIAN

Honor

Better die in honor than live in disgrace.
VIETNAMESE

Do not lose honor through fear.
SPANISH

There is honor among thieves.
ENGLISH

Hoof

You need not look after the hoofs of dead horses.
RUMANIAN

Hope

Hope holds up the head.
SCOTTISH

Hope is a great deceiver.
SLOVAKIAN

Hope is the last thing to die.
MEXICAN

Horn (animal)

When the horns are off, it is too late to butt.
NORWEGIAN

Horn (instrument)

The bigger the horn, the louder the sound.

SLOVAKIAN

Horse

A bad horse eats as much as a good one.

DANISH

A horse is petted just before it is bridled.

SLOVAKIAN

A short horse is soon curried.

ENGLISH

After the horse has been stolen, the stable door is locked.

YIDDISH

Spur not a willing horse.

GERMAN

You can lead a horse to water, but you can't make him drink.

ENGLISH

Hostess

Where the hostess is handsome the wine is good.

FRENCH

Hostility

Hostility does not give birth to a child.

AFRICAN (OVAMBO)

Hot

Soon hot, soon cold.

ENGLISH

Hour

An hour lost is often a year lost.

SWEDISH

Happy hours are very short.

VIETNAMESE

The hours of parting are the warmest.

FINNISH

House

Go not every evening to your brother's house.

SPANISH

If you go into a house, you must know where the exit is.

PHILIPPINE

It is no time to play chess when the house is on fire.

ITALIAN

Keep your house and your house will keep you.

ENGLISH

People in glass houses must not throw stones.

ENGLISH

When you get into a house, follow the rules of that house.

VIETNAMESE

Household

Large household, thin soup.

ESTONIAN

Humility

Too much humility is pride.

GERMAN

Hunger

Go not with every hunger to the cupboard, nor with every thirst to the pitcher.

PORTUGUESE

Hunger is the best cook.

GERMAN

Hunger is the best sauce.

ENGLISH

Hunger teaches you how to chew melon seeds.

AFRICAN (OVAMBO)

Hunter

If a hunter kills a buffalo in the bush, he must bring back a tail.

AFRICAN (SWAHILI)

The hunter pursuing the deer sees not the mountain.

JAPANESE

Husband

A good husband makes a good wife.

ENGLISH

A good husband may have a bad wife, and a bad husband may have a good wife.

INDIAN (TAMIL)

When husband and wife agree with each other, they can dry up the ocean with buckets.

VIETNAMESE

Hut

A hut is a palace to a poor man.

IRISH

Hyena

One does not put a hyena among goats.

AFRICAN (OVAMBO)

Ice
Ice three feet thick is not frozen in a day.
CHINESE

Idleness
Idleness is the devil's workshop.
GERMAN

Idleness is the mother of all evil.
GREEK

Ignorance
Ignorance is bliss.
AMERICAN

Ignorance is more troublesome than poverty.
BURMESE

Illness
Illness comes by many roads but always uninvited.
CZECH

No one buys illness with money.

LATVIAN

Ills

Desperate ills require desperate remedies.

FRENCH

Imitation

Imitation is the sincerest form of flattery.

ENGLISH

Impatience

A little impatience spoils great plans.

CHINESE

Inch

An inch of gold will not buy an inch of time.

CHINESE

Industry

Industry in youth will support one in old age.

INDIAN (TAMIL)

Industry need not wish.

AMERICAN

Ingratitude

Ingratitude is the world's reward.

GERMAN

Injustice
Injustice has no price.
ESTONIAN

Inn
Find your inn before nightfall.
CHINESE

Innkeeper
No one would be an innkeeper but for money.
SPANISH

Insult
Insults are more painful than lashes.
PHILIPPINE

Insult gives birth to insult.
GREEK

Intelligence
Intelligence consists in recognizing opportunity.
CHINESE

Intelligence is not sold for money.
TURKISH

Intention

The camel's intention is one thing, the camel driver's is something else.

LEBANESE

Interest

Interest rules the world.

AMERICAN

Iron

Iron takes iron from the furnace.

IRANIAN

Iron that is not used soon rusts.

PORTUGUESE

Strike while the iron is hot.

ENGLISH

Itch

An itch is worse than a smart.

ENGLISH

Ivory

Ivory does not grow in the mouth of a dog.

CHINESE

Real ivory will not be eaten by insects.

BURMESE

Jack
Every Jack has his Jill.
ENGLISH

Jealousy
Jealousy is the life of love.
JAPANESE

No jealousy, no love.
GERMAN

Job
Do your own job and eat your own fruits.
IRISH

Nothing is too far and no job is too hard if you like it.
PHILIPPINE

Journey

Every journey gives you its own flavor.

LIBYAN

Nothing is lost on a journey by stopping to pray or
to feed your horse.

SPANISH

Joy

After joy comes sorrow.

ENGLISH

Joy and sorrow are next-door neighbors.

GERMAN

Judge

Whoever is judge between two friends loses one of them.

GERMAN

No one is a good judge in his own cause.

PORTUGUESE

Jug

Drop by drop the jug is filled.

GREEK

Like jug, like lid.

ESTONIAN

Jungle

The jungle will not be without a tiger.

PASHTO

Justice

Justice is as the rulers make it.

RUMANIAN

Justice often leans to the side where the purse pulls.

DANISH

Rigorous justice is often injustice.

SLOVENIAN

Kettle

Everybody collects coals under his own kettle.

FINNISH

Key

A golden key fits every door.

POLISH

The used key is always bright.

ENGLISH

Kindness

A word of kindness is better than a fat pie.

RUSSIAN

Kindness breaks no bones.

GERMAN

Too much kindness is of no profit to a child or man.

TURKISH

King

A king without learning is but a crowned ass.

ENGLISH

As is the king, so are his people.

SPANISH

When a king makes a mistake, all the people suffer.

CHINESE

Kingdom

It is easy to govern a kingdom but difficult to
rule one's family.

CHINESE

Kiss

A kiss must last long to be enjoyed.

GREEK

Frequent kisses end in a baby.

HUNGARIAN

Kisses are first, and cusses come later.

MEXICAN

Kitchen

A fat kitchen makes a lean will.

FRENCH

All that is said in the kitchen should not be heard in the parlor.

SCOTTISH

Kite

The kite flies because of the tail.

HAWAIIAN

Knife

A dull knife slaughters no chicken.

AFRICAN (SWAHILI)

One knife whets another.

ITALIAN

Who has no knife, may not eat pineapples.

JAMAICAN

Knowledge

Knowledge is better than riches.

AFRICAN (EFIK)

Knowledge is power.

ENGLISH

Label

Don't rely on the label of the bag.

FRENCH

Labor

As the labor, so the pay.

GERMAN

Labor is bitter, but sweet is the bread which it buys.

INDIAN (HINDI)

Laborer

The laborer is worthy of his hire.

ENGLISH

Ladder

Step after step the ladder is ascended.

ENGLISH

Lake

There is no lake without frogs.

TURKISH

Lamb

The lamb is a sheep in the long run.

IRISH

Where the lamb is sheared, there is the wool.

ESTONIAN

Lamp

Light your lamp before night overtakes you.

GREEK

The lamp of one house cannot light two houses.

CHINESE

Land

Everyone praises his own land.

IRISH

No land without stones, or meat without bones.

ENGLISH

Lane

It is a long lane that has no turning.

ENGLISH

Language

As long as the language lives the nation is not dead.

CZECH

Who knows the language is at home everywhere.

DUTCH

Late

Better late than never.

ENGLISH

Laugh

He who laughs last, laughs best.

ENGLISH

Laugh and the world laughs with you, weep and you weep alone.

AMERICAN

Laughter

Laughter is heard farther than weeping.

YIDDISH

The laughter of a child is the light of a house.

AFRICAN (SWAHILI)

Law

Law makers should not be law breakers.

SCOTTISH

The law turns on golden wheels.

RUMANIAN

The more law, the less justice.

GERMAN

Lawsuit

Everyone is wiser after the lawsuit is ended.

SLOVAKIAN

The first who speaks of lawsuit is not always right.

AFRICAN (WOLOF)

Laziness

Laziness travels so slowly that poverty soon overtakes him.

ENGLISH

What makes the road long is laziness to go.

AFRICAN (BEMBA)

Leaf

Leaves alone don't make a salad.

GERMAN

Leaves have their time to fall.

AMERICAN

Learn

First learn, then form opinions.

HEBREW

No one is too old to learn.

GERMAN

Learning

Learning is a bitter root, but it bears sweet fruit.

CZECH

Learning is a treasure which follows its owner everywhere.

CHINESE

No learning without pain.

SLOVAKIAN

Leg

Better a leg broken than the neck.

DUTCH

Stretch your legs according to your coverlet.

ENGLISH

Lentil

Lentils without onions are like a dance without music.

GREEK

You don't soak lentils in your mouth.

ARMENIAN

Leopard

A leopard does not sleep with a goat.

AFRICAN (ZULU)

The leopard does not change his spots.

ENGLISH

Liar

Liars should have good memories.

ENGLISH

One liar knows another.

IRISH

Lid

Don't lift off the lid too soon.

CHINESE

If there is a lid that does not fit there is a lid that does.

JAPANESE

Lie

If lies were as heavy as stones to carry many would prefer the truth.

SWEDISH

Lies have short legs.

GERMAN

Life

Human life is like a candle.

ALBANIAN

Life has its ups and downs.

AMERICAN

While there's life there's hope.

ENGLISH

Light

The light of a hundred stars does not equal the light
of the moon.

CHINESE

There is more light than can be seen through the window.

RUSSIAN

Lightning

Lightning never strikes twice in the same place.

ENGLISH

Where there is lightning, there is thunder.

GREEK

Lily

Even a white lily casts a black shadow.

HUNGARIAN

Linen
Foul linen should be washed at home.
FRENCH

Lining
There is a silver lining to every cloud.
ENGLISH

Link
One link broken, the whole chain is broken.
GERMAN

Lion
A lion doesn't catch mice.
RUSSIAN

If you live with a lion, wear the skin of a crocodile.
AFRICAN (SWAHILI)

When the lion is dead the hares jump upon his carcass.
ITALIAN

Lip
Sweet-melon lips, bitter-melon heart.
CHINESE

Listen

Listen much and speak little.

LITHUANIAN

The one who listens is the one who understands.

AFRICAN (JABO)

Little

Every little helps.

ENGLISH

Little and often makes a lot in time.

GERMAN

Live

It is hard to live, but it is harder still to die.

ALBANIAN

Live and let live.

ENGLISH

To live is either to beat or to be beaten.

RUSSIAN

Lizard

A lizard suns itself within reach of its hiding place.

AFRICAN (SHONA)

Loaf

Half a loaf is better than no bread.
ENGLISH

The loaf in another's hand is always bigger.
SLOVENIAN

Loafer

Any loafer can get shrimps when the shrimps are plentiful.
HAWAIIAN

Lobster

The young lobster learns his manner of walking from the old lobster.
SLOVAKIAN

Two small lobsters make a big one.
MANX

Lock

Locks and keys are not made for honest fingers.
GERMAN

Log

A crooked log makes a good fire.
FRENCH

The green log is burned with the dry ones.

Long

Long is not forever.

Look (noun)

Looks are one thing, and facts are another.

One look before is better than two behind.

Look (verb)

Look before you leap.

Loss

Even loss can be a profit.

Reckon loss before reckoning gain.

Love (noun)

All is fair in love and war.
ENGLISH

Don't be so much in love that you can't tell when the
rain is coming.
MALAGASY

It is loving too much to die of love.
FRENCH

Love and blindness are twin sisters.
RUSSIAN

Love does not choose the blade of grass on which it falls.
AFRICAN (ZULU)

Love does wonders, but money makes marriage.
FRENCH

Love, grief, and money cannot be kept secret.
SPANISH

Love is a fair garden, and marriage a field of nettles.
FINNISH

Love is blind.
ENGLISH

Love is sweet, but it's nice to have bread with it.

YIDDISH

Love laughs at locksmiths.

ENGLISH

Love makes labor light.

DUTCH

Love will find a way.

ENGLISH

Old love does not rust.

GERMAN

Love (verb)

Love me, love my dog.

ENGLISH

To love and be wise is impossible.

SPANISH

Lover

Lovers think others are blind.

ITALIAN

True lovers are shy, when people are by.

ENGLISH

Loyalty
Loyalty is more valuable than diamonds.
PHILIPPINE

Luck
A little bit of luck is better than a ton of gold.
YIDDISH

Luck and bad luck are driving in the same sledge.
RUSSIAN

When luck offers a finger one must take the whole hand.
SWEDISH

Lying
Lying and gossiping go hand in hand.
SPANISH

Lying pays no tax.
PORTUGUESE

Man (see men)

A drowning man will even clutch at a straw.
RUSSIAN

A lazy man will not bring a hare to market.
AFRICAN (HAUSA)

A man is a lion in his own cause.
ENGLISH

A man is known by the company he keeps.
ENGLISH

A man on his death bed tells no lies.
AFRICAN (SWAHILI)

A wise man carries his cloak in fair weather, and a fool wants
his in rain.
SCOTTISH

A wise man stumbles once over a peg.
PASHTO

Don't kick a man when he is down.
AMERICAN

Every man must skin his own skunk.
AMERICAN

Man does not live by bread alone.
ENGLISH

Man proposes but God disposes.
ENGLISH

No man can serve two masters.
ENGLISH

Take a man by his word, and a cow by her horn.
SCOTTISH

The experienced man is a small prophet.
SLOVENIAN

The man thinks he knows, but the woman knows better.
INDIAN (HINDUSTANI)

The patient man cooks a stone till he drinks broth from it.
AFRICAN (HAUSA)

The wet man fears no rain.
RUMANIAN

The wise man does not hang his knowledge on a hook.

SPANISH

What a sober man thinks, a drunkard speaks.

YIDDISH

When it rains soup the poor man has no spoons.

SWEDISH

Manner

Better good manners than good looks.

IRISH

Look at the manners of others and mend your manners.

JAPANESE

Manure

Manure is the farmer's gold.

ESTONIAN

Mare

Once you have sold the mare you may burn the saddle.

RUSSIAN

Market

If you send no one to the market, the market will send
no one to you.

AFRICAN (YORUBA)

Make the best of a bad market.
SCOTTISH

You must sell as markets go.
ENGLISH

Marriage

Even a good marriage is a time of trial.
RUSSIAN

Marriage and cooking call for forethought.
GREEK

Marriages are made in heaven.
ENGLISH

Marriages are not as they are made, but as they turn out.
ITALIAN

Marriage is heaven and hell.
GERMAN

Marriage without good faith is like a teapot without a tray.
MOROCCAN

More belongs to marriage than four bare legs in a bed.
ENGLISH

Marry

Always say no, and you will never be married.

FRENCH

Marry and grow tame.

SPANISH

Marry in haste, repent at leisure.

ENGLISH

Marrying

Marrying and dying are two things for which one is never late.

YIDDISH

Marrying is easy, but housekeeping is hard.

GERMAN

Master

A bad master quarrels even with his broom.

GREEK

A thousand masters, a thousand methods.

CHINESE

When the master is away the mice play on the table.

RUMANIAN

Meal

A forbidden meal is quickly eaten.
SWEDISH

A meal without salt is no meal.
HEBREW

Measure

Better twice measured than once wrong.
DANISH

Measure seven times, but cut only once.
RUSSIAN

Meat

If you miss the meat, take the soup.
LEBANESE

One man's meat is another man's poison.
ENGLISH

Medal

Every medal has its reverse.
FRENCH

Medicine

Medicine is not roast beef.
MALTESE

There is no medicine against old age.
AFRICAN (YORUBA)

Without measure medicine will become poison.
POLISH

Melon
A melon and a woman are hard to know.
SPANISH

Even a melon seed may come between husband and wife.
IRANIAN

Memory
Memory will slip, a letter will keep.
WELSH

Much memory and little judgment.
FRENCH

Men (see man)
Dead men tell no tales.
ENGLISH

If all men pulled in one direction, the world would topple over.
YIDDISH

Many men, many minds.
CHINESE

Men are all made of the same paste.

RUMANIAN

Men don't all go one road.

MALAGASY

Men trip not on mountains, they stumble over stones.

INDIAN (HINDUSTANI)

Two great men cannot stand side by side.

JAPANESE

Merchant

Every merchant praises his own merchandise.

RUSSIAN

Merchant today, beggar tomorrow.

GERMAN

Mice (see mouse)

It takes a good many mice to kill a cat.

DANISH

Mice cease to fear the cat when she is too old.

BURMESE

Too many mice have no lining for their nest.

AFRICAN (SHONA)

Midwife

Too many midwives kill the baby.

HEBREW

Two midwives will twist the baby's head.

IRANIAN

Might

Might is right.

ENGLISH

Might knows no right.

FRENCH

Milk

After getting burnt on milk, you'll start to blow even on water.

RUSSIAN

To get milk and eggs you must not frighten the cow and hen.

TIBETAN

Mill

Do not set the mill on fire in order to burn the mice.

RUMANIAN

No mill will grind wet corn.

ESTONIAN

The mill that will grind must have water.

WELSH

Miller

Every miller draws water to his own mill.

SCOTTISH

When the miller fights with the chimneysweep, the miller
becomes black and the chimneysweep white.

YIDDISH

Millstone

A millstone gathers no moss.

GERMAN

Mind

A willing mind makes a light foot.

ENGLISH

Careless mind, double work.

GREEK

Minute

Take care of the minutes, and the hours will take care of
themselves.

AMERICAN

Mischief

Everyone is wise when the mischief is done.

SPANISH

Misery

Misery loves company.

ENGLISH

Misfortune

Misfortune comes on horseback and goes away on foot.

FRENCH

Misfortune may turn out to be blessing.

KOREAN

Misfortunes find their way even on the darkest night.

CZECH

One misfortune shakes hands with another.

SWEDISH

Miss

A miss is as good as a mile.

ENGLISH

Mistake

Mistakes will happen.

AMERICAN

The mistakes of others are good teachers.

ESTONIAN

Mistrust

Mistrust is an ax at the tree of love.

RUSSIAN

Mistrust is the mother of safety.

AMERICAN

Mob

The mob has many heads but no brains.

ENGLISH

Modesty

Where there is modesty, there is virtue.

GERMAN

Moment

What the moment broke may take years to mend.

SWEDISH

Money

All complain of their lack of money, none of their want of brains.

RUMANIAN

Better lose a little money than a little friendship.

MALAGASY

Make money honestly if you can, but make money.

AMERICAN

Money and friendship break the arms of justice.

ITALIAN

Money begets money.

ENGLISH

Money comes and goes as the tide ebbs and flows.

VIETNAMESE

Money doesn't tear one's pockets.

LATVIAN

Money is power.

AMERICAN

Money is the sinews of trade.

AMERICAN

Money makes the mare to go.

ENGLISH

Money rules the world.

DUTCH

Money talks.

ENGLISH

When money speaks the world keeps silent.

SWEDISH

With money one can even buy rabbit cheese.

RUMANIAN

Monkey

A monkey remains a monkey, though dressed in silk.
SPANISH

Even a monkey may sometimes fall from the tree.
KOREAN

Monkeys laugh at the buttocks of other monkeys.
JAPANESE

When you see a monkey on a tree it has already seen you.
AFRICAN (FULANI)

Moon

Don't love the moon more than the sun.
THAI

The moon also shines, but does not warm.
RUSSIAN

More

The more the merrier.
ENGLISH

Morning

A misty morning may prove a good day.
SCOTTISH

The early morning is the time to find the people at home.

HAWAIIAN

Morning Hour

The morning hour has gold in its mouth.

GERMAN

Mother

A mother becomes a liar and a thief for the love of her children.

MALTESE

As mother and father, so daughter and son.

GREEK

Every mother thinks her child is beautiful.

YIDDISH

It's the mother who can cure her child's tears.

AFRICAN (HAUSA)

Like mother, like daughter.

ENGLISH

See the mother, and then marry the daughter.

RUMANIAN

Mountain

Behind every mountain lies a vale.

DUTCH

If you don't climb the high mountain, you can't view the plain.

CHINESE

You can't climb a mountain by a level road.

NORWEGIAN

Mouse (see mice)

A mouse can build a home without timber.

AMERICAN

An old mouse does not eat cheese.

MALTESE

It is a bold mouse that makes her nest in the cat's ear.

DANISH

The mouse in its hole is a king.

MOROCCAN

The mouse that knows but one hole is soon caught by the cat.

SPANISH

Mouth

A closed mouth catches no flies.

ENGLISH

If the mouth is fastened shut, no quarrel arises.

JAPANESE

Nothing falls into the mouth of a sleeping fox.

SPANISH

Out of the abundance of the heart the mouth speaks.

ENGLISH

The mouth may talk, but keep your hands busy.

HAWAIIAN

Much

Much would have more.

ENGLISH

Mud

Cast no mud into the well from which you have drunk.

HEBREW

The mud that you throw will fall on your own head.

IRANIAN

Mule

A mule laden with gold is welcome at every castle.

ARMENIAN

Murder

After murder expect justice.

Murder will out.

Music

As the music goes, so goes the dance.

If we pay for the music, we will take part in the dance.

Must

Must is a hard nut.

Nail

Do not hang all on one nail.

GERMAN

Drive the nail that will go.

ENGLISH

Name

A good name is better than fine clothes.

VIETNAMESE

A good name is the root of wealth.

INDIAN (KASHMIRI)

Nature

Nature follows its course and a cat the mouse.

GREEK

Nature passes nurture.

ENGLISH

Necessity

Necessity alters the law.
RUSSIAN

Necessity breaks iron.
DUTCH

Necessity has no law.
ENGLISH

Necessity is the mother of invention.
ENGLISH

Need

Need will have its course.
ENGLISH

The needs of the monkey are not those of the anteater.
AFRICAN (FULANI)

When need is greatest, help is nearest.
GERMAN

Needle

A needle with a piece of string will not be lost.
AFRICAN (HAUSA)

A needle with a small eye should be threaded slowly.
THAI

If a needle can pierce it don't chop with an ax.

BURMESE

It takes a needle to get a thorn from one's foot.

IRANIAN

Negative

Two negatives make an affirmative.

ENGLISH

Neighbor

A near neighbor is better than a distant cousin.

ITALIAN

Better good neighbors that are near than relatives far away.

CHINESE

If your neighbor is an early riser, you will become one.

ALBANIAN

Love your neighbor, but don't pull down the fence.

GERMAN

Your neighbor is your teacher.

EGYPTIAN

Nest

Don't stir up a hornet's nest.
MALAYSIAN

To every bird its nest seems fair.
FRENCH

Net

A new net won't catch an old bird.
ITALIAN

Nettle

Where nettles thrive roses cannot grow.
RUSSIAN

New

The new is always liked, though the old is often better.
DANISH

When the new is there, the old is forgotten.
VIETNAMESE

News

Bad news has wings.
FRENCH

No news is good news.

ENGLISH

The news of a good deed travels far, but that of a bad one farther.

POLISH

Night

Many seek good nights and lose good days.

DUTCH

Night is the mother of plots.

WELSH

Nights of pleasure are short.

LEBANESE

Nightingale

A nightingale cannot sing in a cage.

ENGLISH

Nightingales don't feed on fairy tales.

RUSSIAN

Nobility

Nobility imposes obligations.

FRENCH

Nose

It is better to leave the child's nose dirty than wring it off.

FRENCH

Put not your nose in the pot which doesn't boil for you.

RUMANIAN

Nothing

Nothing will come of nothing.

ENGLISH

There's nothing like trying in this world.

AMERICAN

Nurse

Nurses should not have pins about them.

AMERICAN

Nut

One bad nut spoils all.

AFRICAN (GA)

Oak
Great oaks from little acorns grow.

ENGLISH

Oath
The oaths of one who loves a woman are not to be believed.

SPANISH

Obedience
Willing obedience depends upon him who commands.

PHILIPPINE

Obstacle
Every obstacle is for the best.

GREEK

Ocean

To a fool the ocean is knee deep.

RUSSIAN

The ocean cannot be emptied with a can.

YIDDISH

Oil

When the oil has burned dry, the lamp goes out.

CHINESE

You cannot get oil out of a wall.

FRENCH

Omelet

Omelets are not made without breaking eggs.

ENGLISH

Onion

A dealer in onions is a good judge of scallions.

FRENCH

Keep on peeling an onion and it will disappear.

ARMENIAN

Opinion

Not every opinion is truth.

CZECH

Opportunity

Opportunity knocks only once.

ENGLISH

Opportunity makes desire.

DUTCH

Oppressor

Oppressors sleep not day or night.

INDIAN (TAMIL)

Orange

A rotten orange rots a whole boatload.

MALTESE

A stolen orange is better tasting than your own.

AFRICAN (BEMBA)

Oven

An old oven is easier to heat than a new one.

FRENCH

Owl

The owl is small, its screech is loud.

INDIAN (TAMIL)

The owl thinks all her young ones beauties.

ENGLISH

Owner

An owner of a house knows about its leaking.

AFRICAN (KPELLE)

Ox

An ox and an ass don't yoke well to the same plough.

DUTCH

One blind ox will lead a thousand oxen astray.

INDIAN (KASHMIRI)

One ox can't be sold to two butchers.

LATVIAN

The ox forgets it was once a calf.

SLOVAKIAN

Pain

No pains, no gains.

ENGLISH

Pain is the seed of pleasure.

JAPANESE

Painter

Painters and poets may lie by authority.

ENGLISH

Palm Tree

When you see the palm tree, the palm tree has seen you.

AFRICAN (WOLOF)

Pancake

The first pancake is like a lump.

RUSSIAN

You can't make pancakes without breaking eggs.

SPANISH

Paper

Paper does not blush.

ITALIAN

Paper is patient.

GERMAN

Parents

If you do not support your parents while alive, it is of no use to
sacrifice to them when dead.

CHINESE

Parents are the first teachers of the children.

BURMESE

Parrot

The parrot will utter what it is taught.

INDIAN (TAMIL)

Partridge

The partridge loves peas, but not those which go into the pot
with it.

AFRICAN (WOLOF)

Passion

Hot passion cools easily.

JAPANESE

The best passion is compassion.

JAMAICAN

Past

Consider the past and you will know the future.

CHINESE

Patch

Better a patch than a hole.

WELSH

Path

The middle path is the safe path.

GERMAN

Patience

Begin with patience, end with pleasure.

AFRICAN (SWAHILI)

Patience is a flower that grows not in every garden.

ENGLISH

Patience is an ointment for every sore.

WELSH

Patience makes all hardships light.

ESTONIAN

Patient

It is no time to go for the doctor when the patient is dead.

IRISH

Pay (verb)

He who pays well is well served.

FRENCH

It pays to advertise.

AMERICAN

Peace

A bad peace is better than a good war.

RUSSIAN

If you like peace don't contradict anybody.

HUNGARIAN

In peace do not forget war.

JAPANESE

Peace pays what war gains.

CROATIAN

Peacemaker

A peacemaker often receives wounds.

AFRICAN (YORUBA)

Peacock

A peacock has too little in its head and too much in its tail.

SWEDISH

Pear

Don't shake the tree when the pears fall off themselves.

SLOVAKIAN

The pear falls under the pear tree.

ALBANIAN

Peasant

A peasant between two lawyers is like a fish between two cats.

SPANISH

Where the peasant is poor the whole country is poor.

POLISH

Pebble

One pebble doesn't make a floor.

AFRICAN (HAUSA)

Peddler

Every peddler praises his own needles.

SPANISH

Pen

Pen and ink never blush.
ENGLISH

The pen is mightier than the sword.
ENGLISH

What's been written by pen can't be cut off by an ax.
RUSSIAN

Penny

A penny saved is a penny earned.
ENGLISH

A penny saved is twice earned.
GERMAN

In for a penny in for a pound.
ENGLISH

People

Learn your way from old people.
ESTONIAN

People count up the faults of those who keep them waiting.
FRENCH

Poor people entertain with the heart.
HAITIAN

Some people are born lucky.

AMERICAN

Wealthy people have many worries.

JAPANESE

Pepper

Put not pepper in other people's meals.

RUMANIAN

Perseverance

Perseverance brings success.

DUTCH

Person

A lazy person chews empty coconut shells.

AFRICAN (SWAHILI)

A person without self-control is like a boat without a rudder.

PHILIPPINE

Let each person drive away his own wasps.

JAPANESE

Seven persons don't wait for one.

RUSSIAN

The person who beats the drum must also know the song.

AFRICAN (BEMBA)

Philosopher

Many talk like philosophers and live like fools.

ENGLISH

Physician

Physician, heal thyself.

ENGLISH

Whatever a physician prescribes is a remedy.

INDIAN (TAMIL)

Picture

A picture is worth a thousand words.

AMERICAN

The picture of a rice cake does not satisfy hunger.

JAPANESE

Pig

Give a pig a chair, he'll want to get on the table.

YIDDISH

Let ever pig dig for itself.

MANX

Old pigs have hard snouts.

GERMAN

To lazy pigs the ground is always frozen.

SWEDISH

Pigeon

Pigeon flies with pigeon, hawk with hawk.

IRANIAN

Pill

Bitter pills are gilded.

GERMAN

Pilot

Too many pilots wreck the ship.

CHINESE

Pinch

Pinch yourself to find out how much it hurts others.

PASHTO

Pint

A pint is a pound the world around.

AMERICAN

Piper

They that dance must pay the piper.

AMERICAN

Pitcher

Little pitchers have big ears.

ENGLISH

The pitcher goes often to the well, but is broken at last.

ENGLISH

Place

A charred place smells a long time.

RUSSIAN

A woman's place is in the home.

AMERICAN

It is not good to unpack in an open place.

INDIAN (TAMIL)

There's no place like home.

AMERICAN

Plan

Form your plans before sunrise.

INDIAN (TAMIL)

Plant

Plants often removed never thrive.

GERMAN

Plate

A damaged plate laughs at a broken plate.

AFRICAN (SHONA)

Play

Leave off while the play is good.

SCOTTISH

Turn about is fair play.

ENGLISH

What is play to the cat is death to the mouse.

DANISH

Plea

A plea is always better than a threat.

SLOVAKIAN

Please

If you want to please everybody, you'll die before your time.

YIDDISH

Pleasure

Follow pleasure and pleasure will flee; flee pleasure and pleasure
will follow thee.

ENGLISH

From short pleasure long repentance.

FRENCH

Where there is pleasure there is pain.

JAPANESE

Plough (noun)

The more a plough is used the brighter it becomes.

SLOVENIAN

Plough (verb)

Plough deep while others sleep and you shall have corn
to sell and keep.

ENGLISH

Pocket

Empty pockets, empty promises.

BURMESE

It is too late to spare when the pocket is bare.

GERMAN

Poison

One poison drives out another.

ENGLISH

Politeness

Politeness is not slavery.
AFRICAN (SWAHILI)

Politics

Politics makes strange bedfellows.
AMERICAN

Poor

The poor are cured by work, the rich by the doctor.
POLISH

The poor have their own troubles and the rich their own.
MALTESE

The poor must dance as the rich pipe.
GERMAN

Porcupine

A porcupine will not mind needle grass.
AFRICAN (FULANI)

Possession

Possession is as good as a title.
FRENCH

Possession is nine points of the law.
ENGLISH

Postpone

It is better to postpone than to forget.

ICELANDIC

Pot

A cracked pot will hold sugar.

INDIAN (TAMIL)

A little pot is soon hot.

ENGLISH

A watched pot never boils.

ENGLISH

Small pots soon run over.

SWEDISH

The pot calls the kettle black.

ENGLISH

There is no pot so ugly but finds its cover.

SPANISH

Potter

The potter drinks water from a broken pot.

IRANIAN

The potter knows where to place the handle.

GREEK

Pottery

Pottery and fine porcelain must not quarrel.

C H I N E S E

Poverty

Do not wake poverty when it sleeps.

P O L I S H

Poverty and love are hard to conceal.

N O R W E G I A N

Poverty does not destroy virtue, nor does wealth bestow it.

S P A N I S H

Poverty is no crime.

R U S S I A N

Poverty is the mother of the arts.

S L O V A K I A N

Power

Where the power, there the law.

R U S S I A N

Practice (noun)

Practice makes perfect.

E N G L I S H

Practice makes the master.

G E R M A N

Practice (verb)

Practice what you preach.

ENGLISH

Praise

Little praise is dispraise.

INDIAN (HINDI)

Praise paves the way to friendship.

DANISH

Praising

Praising is not loving.

GERMAN

Present

A present looks for a present.

RUSSIAN

Presents keep friendship warm.

GERMAN

Preserve

Preserve the old, but know the new.

CHINESE

Pretty

Pretty is as pretty does.

AMERICAN

Prevention

Prevention is better than cure.

ENGLISH

Pride

Pride feels no pain.

IRISH

Pride makes the crab go sideways.

JAMAICAN

Pride will have a fall.

ENGLISH

Prison

A prison made of pearls and gold is still a prison.

PHILIPPINE

There is no prison like a guilty conscience.

WELSH

Procrastination

Procrastination is the thief of time.

ENGLISH

Profit

No profit without pains.

Profit and loss are twin brothers.

Small profits are sweet.

Promise

All promises are either broken or kept.

Old promises are left behind.

Promises don't fill the belly.

Proof

The proof of the pudding is in the eating.

Property

Unguarded property teaches people to steal.

Prophet

A prophet is with honor save in his own country.

ENGLISH

Prosperity

In prosperity think of adversity.

DUTCH

Prosperity forgets father and mother.

SPANISH

Prudence

An ounce of prudence is worth a pound of gold.

ENGLISH

Punishment

The best way to avoid punishment is to fear it.

CHINESE

The punishment of one's conscience is heavier than
that of the law.

PHILIPPINE

Puppy

A puppy does not hunt rabbits with a big dog.
AFRICAN (OVAMBO)

A three-day-old puppy does not fear a tiger.
KOREAN

Purse

A light purse makes a heavy heart.
ENGLISH

The purse of the dead man is turned inside out.
GREEK

You can't make a silk purse out of a sow's ear.
ENGLISH

Quarrel

An old quarrel is easily renewed.
ITALIAN

Lovers' quarrels are love redoubled.
PORTUGUESE

The quarrel that doesn't concern you is pleasant
to hear about.
AFRICAN (HAUSA)

Question

Ask no questions and get no lies.
AMERICAN

Don't ask questions about fairy tales.
YIDDISH

Rabbit

If you run after two rabbits, you won't catch either one.

ARMENIAN

When the rabbit has escaped, comes advice.

SPANISH

Race

The race is not always to the swift.

ENGLISH

Rag

If you must be in rags, let your rags be tidy.

IRISH

Rage

Violent rages are soon over.

GREEK

Rain (noun)

After rain comes sunshine.

ENGLISH

Prepare shelter before the rain falls.

PHILIPPINE

When rain beats on a leopard it wets him, but it does not wash out his spots.

AFRICAN (ASHANTI)

Rain (verb)

It never rains but it pours.

ENGLISH

Raindrop

Raindrops will hollow a stone.

KOREAN

Raisin

Every raisin contains a pip.

LIBYAN

Rat

A cornered rat will bite a cat.

JAPANESE

A rat that gnaws pepper is desperate for food.

AFRICAN (ANNANG)

Rats desert a sinking ship.

ENGLISH

Razor

A razor may be sharper than an ax, but it cannot cut wood.

AFRICAN (ANNANG)

Reason

Better die than turn your back on reason.

CHINESE

Who gives many reasons tells many lies.

RUSSIAN

Receiver

The receiver is as bad as the thief.

ENGLISH

Reckoning

Old reckonings breed new disputes.

FRENCH

Reed

A reed need not be afraid when the winds uproot the oak.

POLISH

Refusal

A refusal is better than a broken promise.

WELSH

Regret

A thousand regrets do not pay one debt.

TURKISH

Relation

Love your relations, but live not near them.

ENGLISH

Relations and friends should be visited but not lived with.

SWEDISH

Relative

Eat and drink with your relatives; do business with strangers.

GREEK

Relatives are friends from necessity.

RUSSIAN

Remedy

The remedy is worse than the disease.

ENGLISH

Tomorrow's remedy will not ward off the evil of today.

SPANISH

Remove

Three removes are as bad as a fire.

AMERICAN

Repentance

Repentance is apt to follow haste.

WELSH

There is no repentance after death.

RUSSIAN

Repetition

Repetition is the mother of learning.

RUSSIAN

Repetition teaches the donkey.

LEBANESE

Reputation

A good reputation is a fair estate.

ENGLISH

A good reputation is better than accumulated wealth.

LEBANESE

Resolve

A firm resolve pierces even a rock.

JAPANESE

Respect
Don't have greater respect for money than for man.
VIETNAMESE

Rest
Even rest will make the lazy tired.
HUNGARIAN

Rest makes rusty.
DUTCH

Retreat
A good retreat is better than a poor defense.
IRISH

Revenge
Revenge is sweet.
ENGLISH

The revenge that is postponed is not forgotten.
ICELANDIC

Reward
Reward sweetens labor.
DUTCH

Rhinoceros

Do not speak of a rhinoceros if there is no tree nearby.

AFRICAN (ZULU)

Rice

Rice and fish are as inseparable as mother and child.

VIETNAMESE

There is no burnt rice to a hungry person.

PHILIPPINE

Rich

The rich eat the meat; the poor the bones.

YIDDISH

The rich have many friends.

DUTCH

Riches

Riches adorn the dwelling; virtue adorns the person.

CHINESE

Riches are not the only wealth.

ICELANDIC

Right

Right is a piece of gold which may be cut into strips.
RUSSIAN

Right is a stubborn thing.
AMERICAN

Right makes might.
ENGLISH

Ripe

Soon ripe, soon rotten.
ENGLISH

What ripens fast does not last.
GERMAN

Rise (verb)

Who rises late must trot all day.
AMERICAN

River

It is easy to throw anything into the river, but difficult to take it
out again.
INDIAN (KASHMIRI)

The great river refuses no streamlets.
KOREAN

Where the river is deepest it makes least noise.

ITALIAN

Road

All roads lead to Rome.

ENGLISH

An old road is known.

ESTONIAN

Every road has two directions.

RUSSIAN

The longest road must have an end.

AMERICAN

The road to hell is paved with good intentions.

ENGLISH

Rome

Rome was not built in a day.

ENGLISH

When in Rome, do as the Romans do.

ENGLISH

Roof

The roof of an old hut is always full of leaks.

MEXICAN

Room

When there is room in the heart, there is room in the house.

DANISH

Rooster

The country rooster does not crow in town.

AFRICAN (SWAHILI)

Root

The roots of learning are bitter, but the fruit is sweet.

POLISH

Rope

A rope that is not at hand does not bind the firewood.

AFRICAN (SWAHILI)

Give him rope enough and he'll hang himself.

ENGLISH

Rose

A single rose does not mean spring.

IRANIAN

No rose without a thorn.

ENGLISH

Rule

It is a poor rule that will not work both ways.

AMERICAN

There is no rule without an exception.

ENGLISH

Rum

When the rum is in, the wit is out.

JAMAICAN

Rumor

One rumor breeds another.

SLOVAKIAN

Run

It is not enough to run; one must start in time.

FRENCH

Runner

Where the runner goes the walker will go with patience.

AFRICAN (HAUSA)

Rust

Rust eats iron.

RUSSIAN

Rust wastes more than use.

FRENCH

Sabre

The sabre cuts not its own scabbard.

TURKISH

Sack

A sack is best tied before it is full.

FRENCH

An empty sack won't stand up.

ENGLISH

Saddle

Better lose the saddle than the horse.

ITALIAN

Sage

A great sage is often taken for a great fool.

JAPANESE

Said (see say)
Sooner said than done.
ENGLISH

What's said can't be unsaid.
AMERICAN

Sail (noun)
All sails do not suit every ship.
ICELANDIC

Set your sail according to the wind.
FRENCH

Sailing
It is good sailing with wind and tide.
DUTCH

Sailor
If you are not a sailor, don't handle a boat hook.
CHINESE

Too many sailors drive the boat up the mountain.
JAPANESE

Salt
Salt and bread make the cheeks red.
GERMAN

Salt spilled is never all gathered.

SPANISH

You mustn't pour salt on a wound.

YIDDISH

Salve

There's a salve for every sore.

ENGLISH

Sand

What is written on sand is washed out by the tide.

PHILIPPINE

Sandal

Walk with sandals till you can get good shoes.

LIBYAN

While the sandal is on your foot, tread down the thorns.

HEBREW

Sapling

A sapling becomes an oak.

SLOVENIAN

Sauce

Sauce for the goose is sauce for the gander.

ENGLISH

Sausage
Better a sausage in hand than a ham at the butcher's.
POLISH

Saving
Of saving comes having.
ENGLISH

Say (see said)
Easy to say is hard to do.
FRENCH

Say little and listen much.
GREEK

Saying
Between saying and doing there is a long road.
SPANISH

Scandal
Scandal is like an egg; when it is hatched it has wings.
MALAGASY

Sea
In a calm sea every man is a pilot.
ENGLISH

Smooth seas do not make skillful sailors.
AFRICAN (SWAHILI)

The sea refuses no river.

Season

Everything is good in its season.

Seat

Those who have free seats at the play hiss first.

Secret

A secret stays long in darkness but it will see the light.

Don't tell your secret even to a fence.

The secret of the water pot is known by the ladle.

Security

Security is the first cause of misfortune.

See

Seldom seen, soon forgotten.

Seed

As the seed is, so is the fruit.

RUSSIAN

Unsown seeds will not sprout.

JAPANESE

Seeing

Seeing is believing.

ENGLISH

Seeing once is better than hearing twice.

SWEDISH

Seek

Seek and you shall find.

ENGLISH

Self-Praise

Self-praise stinks.

GERMAN

Self-Preservation

Self-preservation is the first law of nature.

ENGLISH

Sense

Good sense comes only with age.

IRISH

Where sense is wanting, everything is wanting.

AMERICAN

Serpent

A serpent, through it is put in a bamboo tube, won't crawl straight.

KOREAN

The serpent brings forth nothing but a little serpent.

EGYPTIAN

Serve

If you would be well served, serve yourself.

ENGLISH

Shade

There is no shade without a tree.

AFRICAN (SWAHILI)

Shadow

A shadow is a feeble thing but no sun can drive it away.

SWEDISH

Nobody can rest in his own shadow.

HUNGARIAN

Shame

Shame lasts longer than poverty.

DUTCH

Share

Share and share alike.

ENGLISH

Shed

A small shed becomes a house.

AFRICAN (OVAMBO)

Sheep

A little sheep always seems young.

FRENCH

A sheep does not give birth to a goat.

AFRICAN (ASHANTI)

Counting your sheep won't keep the wolf away.

LATVIAN

While the sheep bleats it loses its mouthful.

FLEMISH

You can't skin two hides from one sheep.

ARMENIAN

Shell

The shell is needed till the bird is hatched.

RUSSIAN

Shepherd

A lazy shepherd is the wolf's friend.

WELSH

The shepherd smells of sheep even when he becomes a
nobleman.

GREEK

Ship

Do not load everything into one ship.

GERMAN

Free ships make free goods.

AMERICAN

The ship goes, the port remains.

INDIAN (TAMIL)

Shirt

The shirt is nearer than the frock.

SPANISH

Shoe

Don't throw away your old shoes till you have gotten new ones.

DUTCH

Everyone knows where his shoe pinches.

YIDDISH

If the shoe fits, wear it.

ENGLISH

Only the shoe knows of the hole in the stocking.

POLISH

Shoemaker

Shoemaker, stick to your last.

GERMAN

The shoemaker's child goes barefoot.

ENGLISH

Shop

Keep your shop and your shop will keep you.

ENGLISH

Shore

Who owns the shore owns the fish.

RUSSIAN

Shot

Every shot does not bring down a bird.

DUTCH

Shout

Don't shout till you are out of the woods.

ENGLISH

Shower

April showers bring May flowers.

ENGLISH

Shrimp

A sleeping shrimp is carried away by the current.

PHILIPPINE

Shrimps get broken backs in a whale fight.

KOREAN

Shroud

Shrouds are made without pockets.

YIDDISH

Sickness

It is all one whether you die of sickness or of love.

ITALIAN

Sickness comes on horseback, but goes away on foot.

ENGLISH

Side

Hear the other side, and believe little.

ITALIAN

The attractive side of the merchandise is shown.

RUSSIAN

Sight

Out of sight, out of mind.

ENGLISH

Silence

Silence catches a mouse.

SCOTTISH

Silence gives consent.

ENGLISH

Silence is an admission.

WELSH

Silence is golden.

ENGLISH

Silence is worth a thousand pieces of silver.

BURMESE

Silver

When you go out to buy, don't show your silver.

CHINESE

Sin

A sin confessed is half forgiven.

ITALIAN

Each sin has its own excuse.

CZECH

It is a sin to steal a pin.

ENGLISH

Sin enters laughing and comes out crying.

RUMANIAN

Sin is the canoe that will land you in hell.

HAWAIIAN

Where sin drives, shame sits in the back seat.

SWEDISH

Sing

Not everyone who sings is happy.

MALTESE

Sip

A sip at a time empties the cask.

NORWEGIAN

The first sip of broth is always the hottest.

IRISH

Sitting

Sitting a lot ends by making holes in clothes.

AFRICAN (BEMBA)

Ski

One cannot ski so softly that the traces cannot be seen.

FINNISH

Skill

Without skill you cannot even catch a louse.

RUSSIAN

Skin

Don't sell the skin till you've caught the bear.

DUTCH

The skin is nearer than the shirt.

FRENCH

Sky

No sky without clouds.

RUMANIAN

When the sky falls we shall catch larks.

ENGLISH

Sleep

One hour's sleep before midnight is worth two after.

ENGLISH

Sleep is the best doctor.

YIDDISH

The sleep of kings is on an anthill.

PASHTO

Sleeping

There will be sleeping enough in the grave.

AMERICAN

Slip

Better a slip of the foot than of the tongue.

FRENCH

There's many a slip between cup and lip.

ENGLISH

Smith

By working in the smithy one becomes a smith.

FRENCH

Smoke

Smoke from roasting meat does not irritate the eyes.

AFRICAN (SHONA)

Where there is smoke, there is fire.

ENGLISH

You have to suffer smoke in order to keep warm.

CZECH

Snail

When the snail crawls, its shell accompanies it.

AFRICAN (YORUBA)

Snake

A snake is not killed by its own poison.

LEBANESE

Don't trouble a quiet snake.

GREEK

Kill the snake as well as save the stick.

INDIAN (BIHAR)

The snake that wishes to live does not travel on the highway.

HAITIAN

Snooze

You snooze, you lose.

AMERICAN

Snore

All who snore are not asleep.

DANISH

Snow

No one thinks of the snow that fell last year.

SWEDISH

What lay hidden under the snow comes to light at last.

DUTCH

Soil

If you take care of the soil, the soil will take care of you.

LATVIAN

Soldier

Away from the battle all are soldiers.

GERMAN

The common soldiers do the fighting, and the officers claim the victory.

HEBREW

Something

Something is better than nothing.

GERMAN

Son

Better be a poor man's son than the slave of a rich.

RUMANIAN

Send your son to the marketplace and you shall find out with whom he will associate.

LEBANESE

The son disgraces his father by bad conduct.

AFRICAN (EFIK)

Song

Every song has its end.

SLOVENIAN

The song of the stomach is hard to hear.

AFRICAN (WOLOF)

Sore

Different sores must have different salves.

ENGLISH

Where there is no sore there is no need for a plaster.

FRENCH

Sorrow

Sorrow makes the bones grow thinner.

YIDDISH

Sorrow seldom comes alone.

DANISH

Soul

You can't climb into someone else's soul.

RUSSIAN

Soup

Between the hand and the lip the soup may be spilled.

GERMAN

One cannot make soup out of beauty.

ESTONIAN

Who has been scalded with hot soup blows on cold water.

RUSSIAN

Sow (noun)

A sow prefers bran to roses.

FRENCH

The full sow knows not the squeak of the empty one.

WELSH

Sow (verb)

As you sow so will you reap.

ENGLISH

Spare

Spare well and spend well.

ENGLISH

Spark
A little spark kindles a great fire.
SPANISH

Every spark adds to the fire.
AMERICAN

Sparrow
A sparrow in the hand is better than a pigeon on the roof.
GERMAN

Sparrows who emulate peacocks are likely to break a thigh.
BURMESE

Two sparrows on one ear of corn never agree.
SPANISH

Speak
Speak softly and carry a big stick.
AMERICAN

Speak well of the dead.
ENGLISH

What is long spoken of happens at last.
DUTCH

Speech

Honeyed speech often conceals poison and gall.
DANISH

Speech is silver, silence is golden.
GERMAN

Speed

Speed is only good for catching flies.
YIDDISH

Too much speed breeds delay.
AFRICAN (SHONA)

Spender

Great spenders are bad lenders.
ENGLISH

Spice

The best spices are in small bags.
ITALIAN

Spider

The spider does not weave his web for one fly.
SLOVENIAN

Spirit
A broken spirit is hard to heal.
YIDDISH

Sponge
What is said is said, and no sponge can wipe it out.
GERMAN

Spot
By seeing one spot you know the entire leopard.
JAPANESE

The spot will come out in the washing.
SPANISH

Spring
Defile not the spring from which you may drink.
RUSSIAN

Not every spring becomes a stream.
GERMAN

Spur (noun)
The spur won't hurt where the hide is thick.
AMERICAN

Spur (verb)

Don't spur a willing horse.

ENGLISH

Stain

Stains are not seen at night.

HEBREW

Stair

The stairs are mounted step by step.

TURKISH

Star

Even a small star shines in the darkness.

FINNISH

Start

A good start wins the race.

AMERICAN

Steed

It is too late to lock the stable door when the steed is stolen.

DUTCH

Step

A step over the threshold is half the journey.
WELSH

Step by step one goes far.
DUTCH

Stew

The stew that boils much loses flavor.
SPANISH

Stick

A crooked stick will have a crooked shadow.
ENGLISH

Stitch

A stitch in time saves nine.
ENGLISH

Better a stitch now than ten stitches later.
JAPANESE

Stomach

A full stomach gladdens the heart.
MEXICAN

If you go to sleep with an empty stomach, you will count the beams on the ceiling.
YIDDISH

The full stomach does not understand the empty one.

IRISH

The stomach never becomes full with licking.

ESTONIAN

Stone

A rolling stone gathers no moss.

ENGLISH

By the continual creeping of ants a stone will wear away.

INDIAN (TAMIL)

Constant dropping will wear away a stone.

ENGLISH

If many spit on a stone it becomes wet at last.

ICELANDIC

Not all stones are building stones.

LEBANESE

When a big stone rolls it carries many with it.

NORWEGIAN

Storm

After a storm comes a calm.

ENGLISH

The storm blows over but the driftwood remains.

YIDDISH

Story

A false story has seven endings.

AFRICAN (SWAHILI)

The story is only half told when one side tells it.

ICELANDIC

Stranger

A stranger does not know the back door.

JAMAICAN

Straw

Even old straw may be of use sometime or other.

INDIAN (TAMIL)

The last straw breaks the camel's back.

ENGLISH

Stream

It is hard to swim against the stream.

DUTCH

Strength

Strength is defeated by strategy.

PHILIPPINE

String

If the string is long, the kite flies high.

CHINESE

It is good to have two strings to one's bow.

SCOTTISH

Stroke

Different strokes for different folks.

AMERICAN

Little strokes fell great oaks.

ENGLISH

Studies

No studies are necessary to become a fool.

MEXICAN

Stumble

A stumble may prevent a fall.

ENGLISH

Stump

A low stump upsets the sledge.

FINNISH

Success

Nothing succeeds like success.

Suffering

Suffering is bitter, but its fruits are sweet.

Sun

Make use of the sun while it shines.

The sun is the poor man's blanket.

The sun rises whether the cock crows or not.

The sun shines for all the world.

There's nothing new under the sun.

Sunshine

Not all sunshine warms.

RUSSIAN

Suspicion

Suspicion is the poison of friendship.

FRENCH

Swallow

One swallow does not make a summer.

ENGLISH

The swallow carries spring on its wings.

CZECH

Swan

When you are among the swans you become a swan.

THAI

Sweetheart

Nobody's sweetheart is ugly.

DUTCH

With a sweetheart you can have paradise in a hut.

RUSSIAN

Sweetness

You will never taste sweetness if you do not like bitterness.

ESTONIAN

Sword

A sword does not bend and gold does not rust.

RUSSIAN

Two swords do not enter one scabbard.

TURKISH

Tail

A short tail won't keep off flies.

ITALIAN

If the tail is too long, it will be trampled on.

KOREAN

To a tired mare even her tail seems heavy.

SLOVAKIAN

Tailor

A lazy tailor finds his thread too long.

GREEK

Nine tailors make a man.

ENGLISH

Tale

A good tale is none the worse for being twice told.

ENGLISH

Tell no tales out of school.
GERMAN

Talk (noun)

Much talk, little work.
DUTCH

Talk is cheap but it takes money to buy whiskey.
AMERICAN

Too much talk will include errors.
BURMESE

Talk (verb)

The less you talk, the better off you are.
YIDDISH

Talking

Talking is not like doing.
LEBANESE

Talking will never build a stone wall or pay our taxes.
AMERICAN

Tart

One may tire of eating tarts.
FRENCH

Taste

Everyone to his taste.

ENGLISH

There is no disputing about tastes.

ENGLISH

Teacher

Better than a thousand days of diligent study is one day with a great teacher.

JAPANESE

Tear

A tear in place is better than a smile out of place.

IRANIAN

Teasing

Teasing eventually turns to a quarrel.

BURMESE

Teeth (see tooth)

Do not show your teeth until you can bite.

IRISH

One must chew according to one's teeth.

NORWEGIAN

Temper
Bad temper and anger shorten the years.
YIDDISH

Temptation
Temptation arrives unannounced.
ARMENIAN

Tent
A tent without a wife is like a fiddle without a string.
RUMANIAN

Termite
Small termites collapse the roof.
AFRICAN (OVAMBO)

Thaw
Thaw reveals what has been hidden by snow.
DANISH

Thief (see thieves)
Set a thief to catch a thief.
ENGLISH

There is no thief without a receiver.
SPANISH

Thieves (see thief)

Big thieves hang little ones.

CZECH

When thieves fall out the thefts come to light.

SPANISH

Thing

A thing too much seen is little prized.

FRENCH

Every thing has its time.

ENGLISH

Good things require time.

DUTCH

Things carefully kept are not gotten at by rats.

HAWAIIAN

Things done cannot be undone.

ENGLISH

When a thing is done, don't talk about it.

CHINESE

Think

First think, then speak.

TURKISH

Thinking
Nobody is hanged for thinking.

HUNGARIAN

Thorn
Kicking against thorns will cause pain.

INDIAN (TAMIL)

The youngest thorn is the sharpest.

IRISH

Thought
Second thoughts are best.

ENGLISH

Thoughts are toll free.

GERMAN

Thread
The thread follows the needle.

ENGLISH

Thread by thread the largest robe is woven.

HEBREW

Threat
A threat will not kill.

WELSH

Threshold

The most difficult mountain to cross is the threshold.

DANISH

Thumb

One thumb cannot crush a louse.

AFRICAN (SHONA)

Tide

Every tide will have an ebb.

ENGLISH

The tide may turn.

AMERICAN

Tiger

Don't caress the tiger's whiskers when he is sleeping.

VIETNAMESE

Who rides the tiger finds it difficult to dismount.

CHINESE

Timber

Stolen timber also burns.

RUSSIAN

Time

No time like the present.
English

Other times, other manners.
French

There is a time for all things.
English

There is a time for work and a time for play.
Russian

There is always a first time.
American

Time and money make everything possible.
Maltese

Time flies.
English

Time is money.
English

Time will tell.
American

Today

One today is better than ten tomorrows.
German

Tomorrow

Never put off till tomorrow what you can do today.

ENGLISH

Tone

It is the tone that makes the music.

GERMAN

Tongue

A double tongue will slip.

INDIAN (TAMIL)

A sweet tongue hides a bad heart.

JAMAICAN

Keep guard over the tongue that is in your mouth.

TURKISH

Turn your tongue seven times before speaking.

FRENCH

Tooth (see teeth)

Better a tooth out than always ache.

ENGLISH

Toothache

When a toothache comes, you forget your headache.

YIDDISH

Torch

Do not light a torch from both ends.

AFRICAN (OVAMBO)

Tortoise

The tortoise is not overburdened by its shell.

AFRICAN (SHONA)

Town

If everyone swept in front of his house, the whole town would be clean.

POLISH

Toy

There are toys for all ages.

FRENCH

Trace

That which leaves no trace has done no harm.

ICELANDIC

Trade

Each trade has its own ways.

CHINESE

Trade must regulate itself.

AMERICAN

Two of a trade can never agree.

Trap

A trap without bait catches nothing.

AFRICAN (SWAHILI)

Traveler

Choose your fellow traveler before you start on your journey.

AFRICAN (HAUSA)

Treasure

Treasures laid up in the mind do not decay.

JAPANESE

Tree

A rotting tree leans long before it falls.

FINNISH

A tree bears fruit even if stones are thrown at it.

SWEDISH

Bend trees to the shape you want when they are still young.

VIETNAMESE

Don't cut down the tree to get the fruit.

PHILIPPINE

No tree falls at the first stroke.

One tree does not make a forest.

The tree is known by its fruit.

Trick

A trick is clever only once.

Trouble

Never trouble trouble till trouble troubles you.

The troubles of a stranger aren't worth an onion.

Trout

A trout in the pot is better than a salmon in the sea.

There's no catching trouts with dry breeches.

Trust

Put not your trust in money, but put your money in trust.
AMERICAN

Too much trust breeds disappointments.
PHILIPPINE

Truth

Every truth is not good to be told.
ITALIAN

Tell the truth and shame the devil.
ENGLISH

The truth rises to the surface like oil on water.
SLOVAKIAN

Truth is a lion, and lies are a hyena.
MOROCCAN

Truth is stranger than fiction.
ENGLISH

You can't hide the truth.
RUSSIAN

Tub

Every tub must stand on its own bottom.
ENGLISH

Turn

One good turn deserves another.

ENGLISH

Twig

The twigs are rarely better than the trunk.

ICELANDIC

Young twigs may be bent, but not old trees.

DUTCH

Two

It takes two to make a quarrel.

ENGLISH

It takes two to tango.

AMERICAN

Two can live cheaper than one.

AMERICAN

Two's company, three's a crowd.

ENGLISH

Ugliness

Ugliness with a good character is better than beauty.

AFRICAN (HAUSA)

Umbrella

We remember the umbrella only when it rains.

PHILIPPINE

Union

In union there is strength.

ENGLISH

Use

Use it up, make it do, wear it out, or go without.

AMERICAN

Valley
Who stays in the valley shall never get over the hill.
ENGLISH

Value
The value of prosperity is known by adversity.
AMERICAN

Vanity
Vanity has no greater foe than vanity.
FRENCH

Venison
No one will throw away venison for squirrel's flesh.
AFRICAN (YORUBA)

Venture

Boldly ventured is half won.

GERMAN

Nothing ventured, nothing gained.

ENGLISH

Vessel

A vessel holds only its fill.

IRISH

Empty vessels make the most sound.

ENGLISH

Vice

Vice is learned without a schoolmaster.

DANISH

Vice will not conquer virtue.

INDIAN (TAMIL)

Victor

The victor feels no fatigue.

SLOVENIAN

Victory

Don't divide the spoil before the victory is won.

GERMAN

The only victory over love is flight.

FRENCH

Village

In a village do as the village does.

JAPANESE

The village that is in sight needs no guide.

TURKISH

Vinegar

Free vinegar tastes better than bought honey.

ALBANIAN

Vineyard

Fence your own vineyard, and keep your eyes from
those of others.

GREEK

Violence

If violence comes by the door, law goes out by the chimney.

TURKISH

Violin

It is not with an ax that the violin is played.

WELSH

Virtue

There is no virtue in a promise unless it be kept.
DANISH

Virtue is its own reward.
ENGLISH

Virtue knocks beauty dead.
VIETNAMESE

Visit

Short visits make long friends.
ENGLISH

Visitor

One can't go to bed when a visitor stays late.
BURMESE

Voice

The voice of the ass is not heard in heaven.
RUMANIAN

The voice of the people, the voice of God.
ENGLISH

Vulture

The vulture catches not the fly.
TURKISH

Where there is meat, the vultures congregate.
AFRICAN (BEMBA)

Wage

Whoever takes wages for work must needs perform it.

AFRICAN (FULANI)

Wager

A wager is a fool's argument.

SCOTTISH

Wagon

Empty wagons make most noise.

DANISH

Walk

Before you walk you have to creep.

JAMAICAN

Walker

Even a slow walker will arrive.

AFRICAN (OVAMBO)

253

Wall

It is bad to lean against a falling wall.

DANISH

Walls have ears.

ENGLISH

You can't build a wall with just one stone.

GREEK

Wallet

As the wallet grows, so do the needs.

YIDDISH

Want

For want of a nail the shoe is lost; for want of a shoe the horse is lost; for want of a horse the rider is lost.

ENGLISH

War

War among grasshoppers delights the crow.

AFRICAN (SWAHILI)

War brings peace.

GERMAN

War makes robbers, peace hangs them.

FRENCH

Ware

Good wares make a quick market.

SCOTTISH

Wasp

The wasp makes not honey.

TURKISH

Waste

Waste not, want not.

ENGLISH

Watch

Good watch prevents harm.

SCOTTISH

Water

A very little water is a sea to an ant.

PASHTO

Any water puts out fire.

FRENCH

Don't put water into somebody else's wine.

GREEK

Hot water is no playground for a frog.

AFRICAN (FULANI)

If you want clear water, draw it from the spring.
PORTUGUESE

Muddy water won't do for a mirror.
ITALIAN

Still waters run deep.
ENGLISH

Store up the water while it rains.
BURMESE

Water in peace is better than wine in war.
GERMAN

Water past will not turn the mill.
SPANISH

You never know the worth of water till the well is dry.
ENGLISH

Waterfall
What the waterfall brings the stream carries away.
FINNISH

Watermelon
A watermelon will not ripen in your armpit.
ARMENIAN

Wax

The wax hardens when it's away from the fire.

BURMESE

Way

Better ask twice than lose your way once.

DANISH

If shy to ask, you will lose your way.

MALAYSIAN

The way to heaven is full of obstacles and brambles.

PHILIPPINE

Wealth

The best wealth is health.

WELSH

Wealth can be concealed, but not poverty.

FINNISH

Wealth is a fine thing, but to find an heir is not easy.

AFRICAN (ASHANTI)

Wealth is like smoke.

AFRICAN (FULANI)

Wealth will not keep death away.

WELSH

When there is wealth, there is power.

INDIAN (TAMIL)

Wedding

After the wedding it's too late to have regrets.

YIDDISH

One wedding begets another.

ENGLISH

There is no wedding without laughter and no death without tears.

RUMANIAN

You can't dance at two weddings at the same time!

YIDDISH

Wedge

Hard wedges are needed for hard tree stumps.

NORWEGIAN

One wedge drives another.

GERMAN

Wedlock

Wedlock is a padlock.

ENGLISH

Weed

Ill weeds grow apace.

ENGLISH

Weeds never die.

GERMAN

Well (adverb)

All is well that ends well.

ENGLISH

Well (noun)

A well is not dug with a needle.

ARMENIAN

One does not descend into a well by a rotten rope.

TURKISH

Wheat

No wheat without its chaff.

ENGLISH

Wheel

A turning wheel does not get rusty.

GREEK

Whip

It is enough to show a whip to a beaten dog.

CZECH

Whistle

It isn't every kind of wood that a whistle can be made from.

LATVIAN

Why

Every why has its wherefore.

ENGLISH

Wife

A good wife and health are a man's best wealth.

ENGLISH

A man without a wife is a man without thoughts.

FINNISH

A wife gives beauty to a house.

INDIAN (TAMIL)

Curse not your wife in the evening, or you will have
to sleep alone.

CHINESE

Do not choose your wife at a dance, but on the field among
the harvesters.

CZECH

In a beloved wife there is no evil.

AFRICAN (JABO)

Leave her now and then if you would really love your wife.

MALAYSIAN

Will (noun)

The will is a good horse.

WELSH

The will is the soul of the work.

GERMAN

Where there's a will there's a way.

ENGLISH

Will is power.

FRENCH

Will (verb)

He that will not when he may, when he will shall have nay.

ENGLISH

Willow

Bend the willow while it is young.

DANISH

Wind

It's an ill wind that blows nobody good.
ENGLISH

The wind will fell an oak, but cannot destroy the reed.
HUNGARIAN

Where there is no wind, bushes don't shake.
PASHTO

Wind and fortune are not lasting.
PORTUGUESE

Wine

Good wine makes good blood.
ITALIAN

In wine there is truth.
ENGLISH

Sweet wine makes sour vinegar.
GERMAN

When wine enters modesty departs.
ITALIAN

Who loves not wine, women, and song remains a fool his whole
life long.
GERMAN

Wine in, wit out.
ENGLISH

Wine reveals a person's true heart.

JAPANESE

Winter

The winter asks you what you have done during the summer.

LATVIAN

Wisdom

All wisdom is not taught in your school.

HAWAIIAN

Too much wisdom is folly.

GERMAN

Wisdom adorns old age.

RUSSIAN

Wisdom cannot be bought for money.

AFRICAN (OVAMBO)

Wisdom without use is fire without warmth.

SWEDISH

Wise

Some are wise and some are otherwise.

ENGLISH

You don't' have to be wise to be lucky.

YIDDISH

Wish

If wishes were horses beggars would ride.

ENGLISH

Wishes never filled the bag.

FRENCH

Witness

No witness can become the judge.

HEBREW

Wolf

A wolf and a sheep never agree.

GREEK

Live with a wolf, howl like a wolf.

ESTONIAN

Make yourself a sheep and the wolf will eat you.

FRENCH

Talk of the wolf and his tail appears.

DUTCH

The wolf changes his fur, but never his habits.

RUMANIAN

The wolf loses his teeth, but not his inclinations.

SPANISH

Who keeps company with the wolf will learn to howl.

ENGLISH

Woman (see women)

A beautiful woman is a beautiful trouble.

JAMAICAN

A good woman is worth more than rubies.

PHILIPPINE

A house without a woman is a meadow without dew.

CZECH

A plain woman with moral beauty is better than a beautiful woman.

VIETNAMESE

A pregnant woman wants toasted snow.

HEBREW

A thrifty woman is the wealth of her house.

MALTESE

A woman is attractive when she is somebody else's wife.

AFRICAN (SHONA)

A woman laughs when she can, and weeps when she pleases.

FRENCH

He who marries a woman for her money is good for nothing.

LEBANESE

If a woman is cold, it is her husband's fault.

RUSSIAN

Though a beautiful woman does not say anything, she cannot be hidden.

JAPANESE

Women (see woman)

Among beautiful women there are many fools.

JAPANESE

It is easier to make a hundred watches agree than ten women.

POLISH

Two women in one house will not agree long.

ENGLISH

Women look for talent, men for beauty.

VIETNAMESE

Wood

By the side of dry wood the green will also burn.

SLOVENIAN

Green wood makes a hot fire.

ENGLISH

Wooer

A wooer should open his ears more than his eyes.

NORWEGIAN

Wooing

Happy is the wooing that is not long a-doing.

ENGLISH

Wool

Better lose the wool than the lamb.

GREEK

Word

A good word extinguishes more than a pailful of water.

SPANISH

A harsh word is more painful than a blow.

INDIAN (TAMIL)

A true word needs no oath.

TURKISH

A word to the wise is enough.

ENGLISH

Fair words butter no parsnips.

ENGLISH

Kind words don't wear out the tongue.

DANISH

Many a true word is spoken in jest.

ENGLISH

One word in its place is worth a camel.

LEBANESE

Pleasant words will draw a snake from its hole.

AFRICAN (SWAHILI)

Words are mere bubbles of water, but deeds are drops of gold.

TIBETAN

Words once uttered cannot be overtaken even by a
four-horse coach.

KOREAN

Work

A woman's work is never done.

ENGLISH

All work and no play makes Jack a dull boy.

ENGLISH

The hard work of a hundred years may be destroyed in an hour.

CHINESE

The work praises the workman.

GERMAN

Work is the mother of life.

SLOVAKIAN

World

Half the world knows not how the other half lives.
ENGLISH

Take the world as it is, not as it ought to be.
GERMAN

The world befriends the elephant and tramples on the ant.
INDIAN (HINDUSTANI)

The world holds more for the healthy than the wealthy.
SLOVAKIAN

The world is wide, yet there is little room in it.
POLISH

Worm

Tread on a worm and it will turn.
ENGLISH

Worms eat you up when dead and worries eat you up alive.
YIDDISH

Worry

Worries about children continue until death.
LEBANESE

Worries are easier to bear with soup than without it.
YIDDISH

Wound

A wound heals but bad words never fade.
PHILIPPINE

The wound heals, the scar remains.
CROATIAN

Wrong

Two wrongs will not make one right.
ENGLISH

Year

What does not happen in a year may happen in a moment.

SPANISH

Years and months are like a flowing stream.

JAPANESE

Youth

What you learn in youth you do not unlearn in old age.

GREEK

Youth has a beautiful face and old age a beautiful soul.

SWEDISH

Youth may stray afar yet return at last.

FRENCH

Youth will have its fling.

ENGLISH

Zeal

Too much zeal spoils all.

FRENCH

Zeal without knowledge is fire without light.

ENGLISH